EMBROIDERING *within* BOUNDARIES

Afghan Women Creating a Future

By RANGINA HAMIDI & MARY LITTRELL   Photos by PAULA LERNER

THRUMS
BOOKS

Editor/Publisher: *Linda Ligon*
Associate Publisher: *Karen Brock*
Design: *Susan Wasinger*

306 North Washington Avenue
Loveland, Colorado 80537
USA

Printed in China by Asia Pacific
Library of Congress Control Number 2017933269

For our fathers,
Ghulam H. Hamidi and Herbert H. Bishop,
who encouraged and supported our education.

Acknowledgments

The International Folk Art Alliance (IFAA), based in Santa Fe, New Mexico, has played an important role in our lives. We are grateful to CEO Jeff Snell, his leadership team, and the IFAA Board of Directors for their work toward celebrating and preserving living folk arts around the world. Together with artists, IFAA is creating economic opportunities and laying the groundwork for artists to serve as catalysts for social change in their communities. In particular, we thank Judy Espinar, a co-founder of the International Folk Art Market-Santa Fe, for her longtime support of Kandahar Treasure and for her encouragement in telling the story of Kandahar Treasure.

From RANGINA

The birth of Kandahar Treasure would not have been possible without guidance provided by Project Artemis at Arizona State University's Thunderbird School of Global Management and Business Council for Peace (BPeace). The foundation of Kandahar Treasure is built on business training provided by both institutions whose knowledge, support, and commitment transformed a dream into a reality.

A special thanks to Catherine Shimony, co-founder of Global Goods Partners, who shares my passion for women and crafts around the world. She not only carries our unique products to sell online but continues to provide advice and practical ideas to sustain and support Kandahar Treasure, helping us to produce new and competitive products for the handmade market.

I would like to thank my co-author Mary Littrell who graciously offered to write our story—many people had

Acknowledgments *(continued)*

heard our story; she chose to write it! Thanks also to all of my colleagues in Kandahar who work under dire conditions to make Kandahar Treasure a success. Without their commitment and hard work, we would not have this book today. To Toni Maloney of BPeace for helping me craft the name Kandahar Treasure and to Athena Katsaros and Kate Buggeln for wanting to be my mentors and for becoming my friends. To Kellie Kreiser who continues to be the angel that Kandahar Treasure needs to make new connections and to become involved in new opportunities. To Nadia Aman and Palwasha Lena Kakar for their belief and unending support to me and to Kandahar Treasure.

I am who I am because of my loving family. My caring parents and my amazing sisters and soulmates, Farida, Wazma, Stoorai, and Zarmina, have cleared all boundaries for me. You have always been there for me and have enabled me to reach my dreams in ways unimaginable to many other young Afghan women. I am grateful for having you all in my life.

Finally, to my husband Abdullah and to my daughter Zara, for their love, patience, and understanding for my busy traveling life and for my commitment to working wee hours into the night to make Kandahar Treasure a success. I know that I have compromised a lot of our time together. Your love and your unending support and understanding enable me to do the good that I can in this world. Thank you.

From MARY

As this writing project evolved, a number of colleagues came forward to offer their encouragement for telling the Afghan embroiderers' story. These individuals with common interests in global textiles included Judi Arndt, Linda Carlson, Mary Lynn Damhorst, Jana Hawley, Marilyn Murphy, Elena Phipps, Keith Recker, Sylvia Seret, and Clare Smith. My heartfelt thanks go out to each of you.

I am very fortunate to share my life with John Littrell who encourages my work with artisan groups around the world. Even when contemplating a trip to Afghanistan, he trusted that I would make good judgments about travel safety in a country still undergoing political turmoil. As an excellent writer, he willingly reads all that I write and offers excellent critique. This story of women in Kandahar has benefited greatly from his insights and suggestions. Thank you for your collaboration in honoring the work of women in Afghanistan.

TABLE *of* CONTENTS

PREFACE
Our Writing Journey

Stunned silence hung over the audience as Rangina Hamidi concluded her lecture. Immediately, audience members at the 2014 Textile Society of America Symposium waved their hands to be called upon. Their questions confirmed that they had heard an astonishing story. Rangina had shared the account of how 300 members of Kandahar Treasure, a woman-owned business in war-torn Kandahar, Afghanistan, were bravely crossing cultural boundaries to support and create change for their families. Of pivotal importance to the many-layered story—textiles! Yet Rangina's talk contrasted sharply with news from Afghanistan. Journalists and local observers reported that despite thirty years of war, women still maintained little control over their lives in this deeply patriarchal society.

A final statement from a member of the audience set this book in motion. A woman challenged Rangina, "This story of courage has to be told. You have to write a book!" Wild applause reinforced the woman's request. Rangina responded, "I'm not a writer. My work is with the women of Kandahar Treasure."

Sitting in the audience that day, I thought of my own work. Over the past thirty-five years, my life as an academic researcher had focused on how artisan enterprises achieved sustainability in an increasingly competitive global market for handmade goods. I had explored factors contributing to organization vitality and chronicled benefits artisans accrued from their participation. While my books and articles offered portraits of best practices in a variety of settings, none centered on artisans who worked under constant fear from wartime violence. Questions arose in my mind about both the women who work on a daily basis at the workshop and about those who work at home and return their finished products intermittently to the office. With their lives in danger, what motivates these women to leave their compounds and walk considerable distances to Kandahar Treasure? How do the women work and prosper in a country where menfolk rule their lives and forbid them to leave their homes unaccompanied? Clearly Kandahar Treasure offered rare and unique insight into the role textiles could play as catalysts for social change in women's lives.

Rangina had an inspiring story to tell. I possessed the requisite writing tools. Why not collaborate on a book? I approached Rangina; she agreed enthusiastically! Straightaway we embarked on our writing journey. I was already familiar with the stunning khamak embroidery that embellished Afghan men's shirts and brides' trousseaux. For eleven summers, Rangina had displayed the textiles of Kandahar Treasure at the rigorously juried International Folk Art Market in Santa Fe, New Mexico. As a member of the selection jury, I had visited the Kandahar Treasure booth each summer, learning from Rangina how khamak textiles and Afghan identity intertwined. I had also established that this intricate embroidery, with as many as seventy or more stitches per inch, and its prominence in Afghan culture, had not been documented in the textile literature.

Over the next two years and across many hours of discussions between us, the story of Kandahar Treasure unfolded. Hamidi family members added their perspectives. We examined family photos for insights on textile use. In order to understand textile change over time, we pored over several private collections of khamak embroidery dating back to the 1970s. Publications by journalists and aid workers helped place Kandahar Treasure's founding and growth in a socio-political context. How writers inside and outside Afghanistan assessed the impacts of the Russian invasion, Taliban rule, post-9/11 global involvement, national rebuilding, and continuing insurgency in the mid-2000s proved useful.

In the fall of 2015, Rangina encouraged me to travel to Kandahar to experience Afghanistan on the ground. Linda Ligon, our publisher, accompanied me on the trip. Inside Kandahar Treasure's walled compound, we listened attentively to women as they shared their individual stories. The women, ranging in age from eighteen to sixty years, talked of how khamak was used across the lifespan. They emphasized how embroidering for Kandahar Treasure brought calmness to their lives and helped them achieve a measure of economic independence in their homes. We observed the busy workshop where women embroidered while sitting together on the floor or sewed finished products on modern machines. A stream of women who embroidered at home arrived each day to submit finished work, receive payment, and gather new fabric for future projects. In the afternoons, Rangina, Linda, and I visited women in the walled compounds of their homes. As we sat in rooms designated for receiving female guests, women of the households—sometimes as many as twenty mothers, daughters, sisters, aunts, and grandmothers squeezed together—served tea and joined in lively conversations.

In a book on textiles and their makers, visual images are critical in bringing the authors' written words to life. Many of the stunning photographs in this book are the contribution of the late photojournalist Paula Lerner. Rangina collaborated with Paula on projects during Paula's trips to Afghanistan in 2007 and 2009. Prior to Paula's death in 2012, she arranged for her papers and photographs to be donated to the Schlesinger Library at Harvard University. She hoped that other writers could continue her unfinished work in Afghanistan. We are the recipients of Paula's generosity.

As Rangina and Paula worked together, they chose not to minimize the misery in the lives of Afghan women. However, the pair also aspired to portray the joy in women's everyday experiences of baking bread, playing with children, eating in family groups, dancing at wedding receptions, and embroidering khamak. Their joint vision of presenting a balanced and multi-layered perspective of Afghan women inspired and guided us throughout our writing. When women's faces are pictured in the book, it is with their permission. In other cases, we have respected women's requests that their faces not be shown.

As we considered potential publishers for *Embroidering Within Boundaries*, Thrums Books, a publishing company "dedicated to preserving the narrative of traditional textiles and their makers," came immediately to mind. After a long career as Founder and President of Interweave Press, Linda Ligon shepherded a new publishing company. Thrums Books is recognized for publications that integrate deep content about contemporary textile artists with beautiful photos. To our delight, Linda accepted our book prospectus and has guided us enthusiastically along the way. Thank you, Linda, for joining the team in bringing the women of Kandahar Treasure and their exquisite textiles to life.

MARY LITTRELL

Santa Fe, New Mexico
2016

We stitch a tradition, hold the future in our hands.

We strive for peace
and find strength in each other.

We know love and laughter in small moments.

We are nourished by hope.

We live in possibility.

ONE

EMBROIDERING *within* BOUNDARIES

*Attributes (of peasant-tribal societies) perpetuate
an inward-looking society where man is
born into a set of answers.*

Louis Dupree, *Afghanistan*

Afghan women wake each morning surrounded by boundaries in their lives. Viewed as a liability in this deeply patriarchal society, women remain dependent on men. Economic reliance has led women to adhere to their menfolk's *set of answers* as a guide to their actions. At home, the walled compound encloses women's daily activities. They leave only when their fathers, brothers, husbands, fathers-in-law, or sons allow. Most have been denied access to schooling or income-earning opportunities outside the home. On the street, women's voluminous burqas shroud their identities from male scrutiny. By remaining out of sight and conducting themselves in a shy and quiet manner, women bring honor and dignity to their household and lineage. Yet their voices are ignored, and autonomy as women does not exist.

An Internet search of the words, "Afghanistan, the worst place in the world to be a woman," reveals an abundance of government surveys, foundation reports, and accounts from Afghan women journalists confirming this assessment. The Human Development Index (HDI), published annually by the United Nations Development Programme, offers a composite national measure of achievement based on three indicators of human development: a long and healthy life based on life expectancy at birth, access to knowledge grounded in years of schooling, and a decent standard of living gauged by gross national income per person. Of the 188 countries measured in 2015, Afghanistan ranked number 171. Nearly 46 percent of Afghanistan's population lives in or near multidimensional poverty due to acute deprivations in education, healthcare, and living standards (water, electricity, cooking fuel, toilet facilities).

Closer examination of the UN indicators by gender presents a bleak outlook for Afghan women. While women have a slightly longer life expectancy than men (61.6 to 59.2 years), their education and income fall short. In 2015, women over age twenty-five had attended an average of 1.2 years of school, compared to 5.1 years for men. Women earned $506, while men made $3,227 per capita.

Having a man—even a very small man—to accompany women in public provides security and propriety.

Tending livestock, watching
after children, preparing meals,
and making a home keep
Afghan women at the limits of
their energy and resources.
OPPOSITE: *When Nargisa's
young husband was killed in
conflict, she married his brother according to custom. His
death then left her with four
children and responsibility for
extended family members. Her
story is on page 32.*

In the aggregate, Afghan women have achieved a level of human development that is 60 percent of men's level—this in a country where education and economic attainment are already low.

What do these figures of poverty and gender inequality mean for daily life among Afghan women? In a country wracked by three decades of political, social, and economic turmoil, Afghan women face hardships, insecurity, and anxiety across multiple aspects of their lives. For a girl who has not yet reached age sixteen, she may be among the six out of ten girls in her age group who are already married. If she started school prior to marriage, further attendance will be denied. As a young teenage wife, she and her children face likely health traumas as she bears children in a child's body. Access to quality healthcare is grossly inadequate. Although a woman will have on aver-

age six live births, the risks of death are high for a young mother or for her children before age five. Expected by her husband and the larger society to give birth to male children, the pressure to produce boys will continue until she bears a male infant, or better still, multiple sons, over time.

Afghan women's hardships are exacerbated if they are among the country's 1.5 million widows, one of the highest proportions to total population among the world's nations. For more than thirty years, women have lived in fear that the lives of their husbands will be taken in the armed conflicts scarring the country. Teenage wives also face widowhood as older husbands die sooner than their child brides. Once a widow, women no longer have the social protection or economic support of a male. As Afghan journalist Zaghuna Kargar described, "People in Afghanistan don't see widows as human beings who have rights

anymore. Losing a husband is not only about the pain of losing someone you love or someone very close to you. It is the pain of losing almost every freedom you have as a married woman."

To further compound their situation, widows' opportunities for remarriage are limited. A brother of the deceased husband presents the most common option, but then often she will be a second or third co-wife. Should a widow marry outside her deceased husband's family, she stands to lose custody of her children. Afghan widows, at an average age of thirty-five, illiterate, and with more than four children, encounter immeasurable hurdles to provide for their children. Some widows, their lives dissolving into days of desperation, resort to begging on the street.

Irrespective of a woman's age or marital status, her days are consumed by caring for children, baking bread, preparing meals, washing clothes, cleaning, and tending to animals kept within the compound. Husbands and in-laws commonly inflict emotional and physical abuse, given women's low status in the household. Abused women are

Bread, baked daily, is at the heart of Afghan cuisine. Here, a woman prepares special loaves for the celebration of Eid, which ends the annual fasting period of Ramadan.

Burqas, worn only outside of the home, provide women with privacy and security and are necessary for their honor and that of their menfolk.

consistently denied their constitutional rights designed to protect them from domestic violence. Mental healthcare and centers for traumatized women are virtually non-existent. Should a woman want her daughters to attend school, she typically will meet resistance from her husband, father-in-law, and brothers-in-law. As a woman with limited or no schooling and in a culture that prohibits women from appearing in public, the Afghan woman knows little about options for her life. She has few skills and little time for generating sustainable income outside the home. Boundaries restrict and engulf her life in many ways.

WOMEN'S LIVES and TEXTILES CONVERGE

Embroidered boundaries enclose the fine decorative filling stitches of Kandahari women's khamak embroidery. And embroidery is the one sphere of women's lives that men do not control. Its precision, delicacy, and beauty stand in stark contrast to the imperatives of a typical Afghan woman's life. Though the technique is basically a simple satin stitch, the way it is employed in Kandahari textiles is unique and stands with the finest embroidery techniques the world has known. Across generations of Kandahari families, khamak textiles are shared as expressions of love—sister to brother, mother to child, wife to husband, and daughter to parents. Through adorning the body and decorating the home with khamak textiles, Kandahari people honor their families and express pride and identity with their Pashtun culture.

Across Afghanistan's decades of violence, lives have been disrupted. Little time or energy has remained for passing down cultural traditions. As roads and buildings have collapsed to rubble, Afghan traditions have deteriorated. Aesthetics of khamak's fine stitchery and intricate patterns have largely been lost. Creating beauty and maintaining artistic traditions have not been priorities during wartime conflict. This book sheds light, for the first time, on the role that the revival of khamak embroidery during the 21st century is playing in a country working to create stability in the lives of its people.

Despite their cultural significance in Afghanistan, khamak textiles are little known outside the country. Kandahar residents describe the khamak embroidery style as centuries old. Reference to the word *khamak* in published textile books proves elusive. Scholars assert that a pan-Afghan embroidery style does not exist; rather, across time, each of the country's diverse ethnic groups has created its own characteristic embroidery style. Published photographs of Afghan garments from the 1930s and 40s and descriptive text point to men's shirts and women's shawls embellished with extremely fine, white-on-white satin stitch embroidery as a "style of the Pashtun people of Kandahar." Authors describe the illustrated Kandahari men's shirt fronts as "magnificent"

with their embroidered "Pashtun satin stitches." These photos correspond closely with contemporary embroidery produced among Kandahari Pashtun women, speaking to a tradition that has somehow managed to survive and been reborn.

KANDAHAR TREASURE, RECLAIMING HISTORY

The revival of khamak embroidery focuses on the untold story of the pioneering women of Kandahar Treasure, an artisan organization in conflict-battered Kandahar, a city considered the home of the Taliban movement in southern Afghanistan. Kandahar Treasure was founded with the goal of creating links among the revival and production of textiles, income generation, and women's attainment of basic human rights in a Muslim society.

Kandahar Treasure provides work for culturally home-bound women, an important first step in securing their economic independence. One-third of the women working with Kandahar Treasure are widows or heads of households. The organization operates from the premise that women's value in the household rises when they contribute financially in caring for themselves and their children. As Carmella Padilla, international folk art authority, notes, "In Afghanistan, when decades of war wipe out venerable examples of cultural art, sales of embroidered textiles help resurrect an artistic tradition and restore pride in women who carry on the tradition." Today, more than 300 women embroider khamak within aesthetic and cultural boundaries as they create new answers for their lives.

In telling the story of Kandahar Treasure, we reflected on a series of questions to guide our exploration—questions such as: *To whom is khamak important? How has the tradition evolved? Why form an enterprise centered on embroidery? How does a women's enterprise operate given the many cultural and religious limitations on women's lives? Is khamak making a difference to the women of Kandahar Treasure? Are the women redefining the boundaries for their lives?* To answer these questions, we've organized the book into three parts.

The first three chapters create context for understanding the lives of Kandahar Treasure women and highlight the importance of khamak-embroidered textiles in the lives of Pashtun people. Across these chapters, we enlarge upon the literal boundaries that define women's lives in Pashtun culture with its strict code of honor, and reflect on how their embroidery serves as a metaphor for living creatively and finding meaning within those boundaries. We look at the role khamak-embroidered garments and household textiles play as cultural markers for Afghan families—both in Kandahar and more broadly within the Afghan diaspora.

The next three chapters tell the story of Kandahar Treasure and its women embroiderers. In these chapters we chronicle Rangina Hamidi's journey to establish Kandahar Treasure—beginning with her family's flight to Paki-

Tiny stitches, counted meticulously, form the foundation of khamak embroidery.

KANDAHAR TREASURE

كندهارى خزانه

MADE IN AFGHANISTAN

KHAMAK : WORKS OF HONOR AND LOVE

www.kandahartreasure.com

Stitching Hopes and Dreams

This shop was located at the U.S. military base in Kandahar, and provided strong sales of khamak goods, a popular gift item for soldiers returning home. It was closed in 2014 when the U.S. withdrew troops from Afghanistan.

*We give voice to women
who are actively creating change
in their lives.*

stan, their immigration to the U.S., her return to her homeland to manage an income-generating project, and later discovering a resolution to find a way to help rebuild Afghanistan by founding the first women-run business in Kandahar Province.

We examine stages in Kandahar Treasure's evolution, and discuss strategies that the organization has employed to work within a conservative Muslim culture and to navigate continuing conflict and insecurity while building a sustainable artisan organization.

Not least, we introduce the technique of khamak stitching itself and look at innovations in the revival of khamak as a living textile tradition.

The final two chapters provide an assessment of challenges, successes, and the future for Kandahar Treasure. We place Kandahar Treasure's evolution within broader frameworks of social entrepreneurship and discuss factors impinging on Kandahar Treasure's long-term organizational sustainability. We give special consideration to the implications for Afghan widows working with Kandahar Treasure.

Throughout, you'll find the stories of women whose lives have been transformed by Kandahar Treasure. We give voice to women who are actively creating change in their lives. Together the women provide their own accounts of their journeys to revive a tradition of beautiful textiles during violent warfare, to make a living from their work, to take control over their lives and those of their children, and to redefine their boundaries.

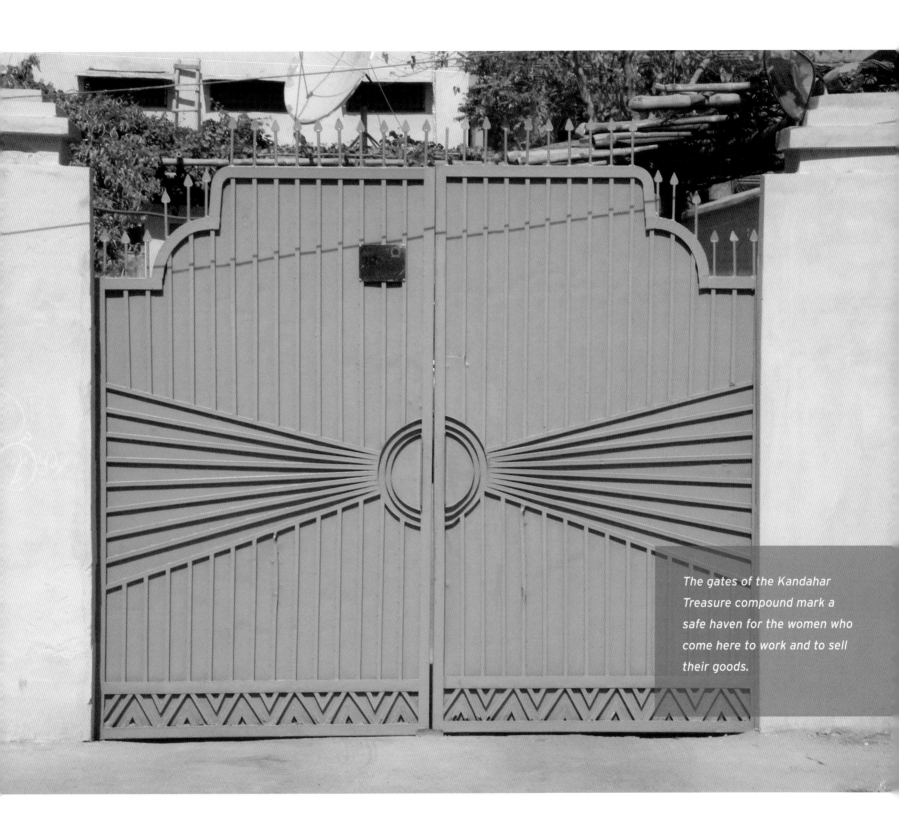

The gates of the Kandahar Treasure compound mark a safe haven for the women who come here to work and to sell their goods.

BRICK
by BRICK

Nargisa's story

As with many Afghan families, Nargisa heads a household that has lost menfolk during the war and has embraced children orphaned by family misfortunes. Nargisa's first marriage lasted one month; her young husband died at the hands of the Taliban. Following Pashtun custom, she then married her brother-in-law. With her second husband she bore four children, all of whom are still young. The children knew their father for only a short time, as he too died in Taliban combat. The oldest daughter, in her teens and pregnant, has returned to the household after a divorce. The soon-to-be-born infant likely will be returned to her former husband; he retains legal right to the baby even though they are divorced. The remaining three children include a teenage boy with developmental

Fabric adorned with hand-stitched embroidery is fundamental to a proper Kandahar home, from the most humble to the elegant.

disabilities and two younger daughters, ages eleven and
twelve. Nargisa also provides a
home to two orphans. One, a tiny
five-year-old boy, was one of trip-
lets whose mother could not care
for her three infants. The mother
kept the two strongest babies and
Nargisa is rearing the third child,
whose small body suggests de-
layed growth. She is also caring

Nargisa's daughters have their own private playhouse, hand-built with mud by their mother's hands. Nargisa takes care that her daughters aren't tempted to play outside the compound, where life can be dangerous.

for her late sister's daughter. The father remarried and the stepmother did not want the child.

Nargisa's small compound of uneven outer walls, two inner rooms, and a rutted dirt courtyard attests to the story of its construction for her family of seven. For many years, Nargisa embroidered khamak and sold it in the neighborhood wherever she could to support her family. A small revenue stream from a few khamak sales continues. After some time, she secured a job as a cleaning lady in the Department of Women's Affairs. Nargisa earns 5,000 afghanis ($73 US) per month, 1500 afghanis ($14 US) of which goes for her bus transportation to work. Somehow, across the years, she managed to save 60,000 afghanis ($875) to buy the land for her house on the far outskirts of Kandahar.

Nargisa's daughters have a large family of homemade dolls–and one Barbie. Of course, they are properly covered with hijabs, which the older girls also wear.

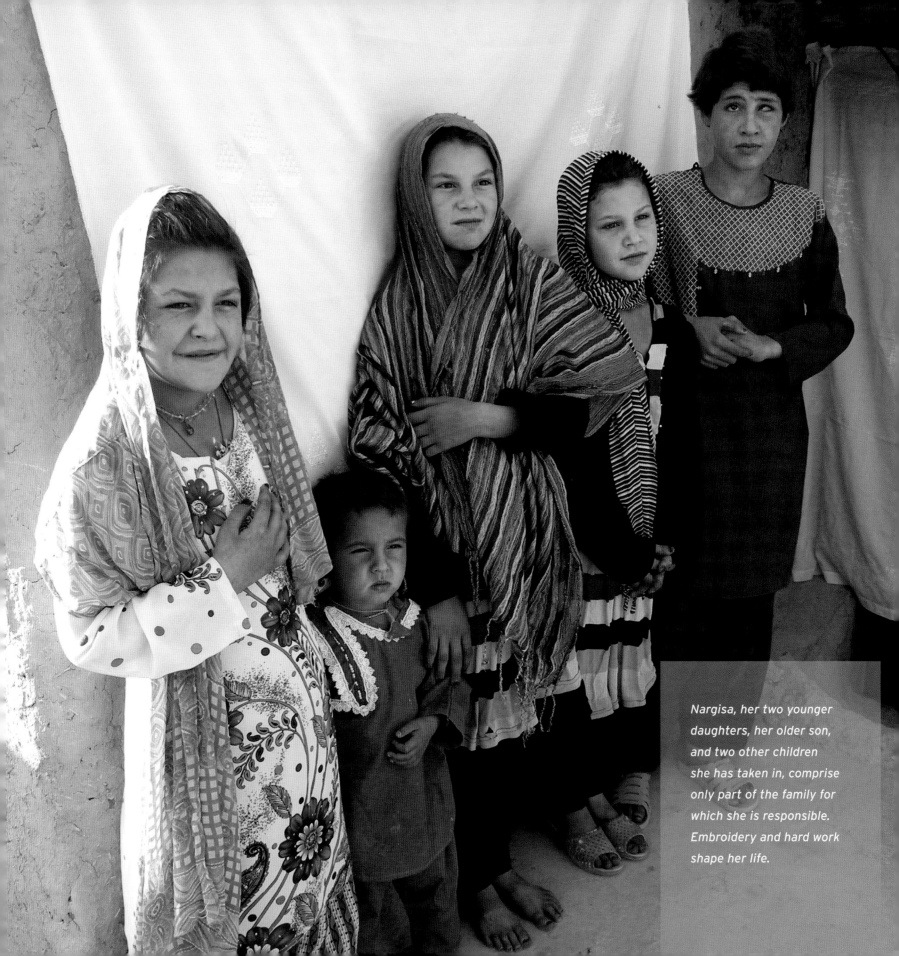

Nargisa, her two younger daughters, her older son, and two other children she has taken in, comprise only part of the family for which she is responsible. Embroidery and hard work shape her life.

At first the family lived in a tent. Upon returning home in the evenings Nargisa would collect water and make adobe for building the compound walls and the rooms where the family resides. In one room, the green and white textiles of Nargisa's embroidered wedding trousseau from many years ago cover the walls and storage trunks. Across the courtyard, a string of crooked poles holds up the jerrybuilt wiring that brings electricity into the house. The young girls have commandeered a walled-off section of the courtyard for their playhouse. The girls giggle as they arrange their dollhouse and dress stick dolls in fabric scraps. A shelf holds an array of used cosmetic containers for a pretend beauty parlor. (The mirror and beauty supplies replicate the establishments where women have their hair elaborately curled and make-up applied prior to attending women-only wedding receptions.)

As we sat in the courtyard with juice drinks, Nargisa brought out framed photos of her two husbands. The children gathered close around to peer into the photos of men they barely knew. Nargisa talked of her life, work, and worries. Somehow, under what seem insurmountable physical, economic, and social conditions, she has garnered the strength and resources to provide her children with a place to live. Spending time with Nargisa, watching her children play, and learning of her life as a mother to six children added poignancy to her earlier welcoming greeting when we first arrived, "This is our home. I built it brick by brick."

TWO

PASHTUN CULTURE *and* BOUNDARIES *in* WOMEN'S LIVES

Your eyes aren't eyes.
They're bees.
I can find no cure for their sting.

A contemporary landay

Afghanistan is a diverse country with many tribal ethnic groups. While current politics dispute the actual percentages, it is accepted by scholars that Pashtun is the largest ethnic group in Afghanistan and in the province of Kandahar, home to Kandahar Treasure.

PASHTUNWALI

Pashtuns follow an ethical code and traditional life-style known as *Pashtunwali*. The system of non-written law and governance began during prehistoric times and is preserved and followed today, mostly in the tribal areas. Pashtunwali is commonly interpreted as "the way of the Pashtuns." The code is so dominant that multiple generations of non-Pashtuns living in majority-Pashtun areas adopt this way of life and culture. Pashtunwali is practiced by Pashtuns in Afghanistan, Pakistan, and by Pashtun refugees around the world. Although Pashtunwali pre-

dates Islam, the code and Islam have become inseparable for many Pashtuns. While there are many primary and secondary codes that govern every aspect of Pashtun life, several principles are key to Pashtunwali behavior.

Melma palana (hospitality). Melma palana requires that Pashtuns accept and admit all visitors, even strangers, to their private homes if asked. Hosts must feed, house, and make guests comfortable before asking who they are and why they are there. Guests are afforded the host's protection, and while in the care and company of a host, guests should neither be harmed nor surrendered to an enemy. Hospitality and protection must be offered without expectation that the favor will be returned. This often has an impact on the women of a family, whose job it is to feed and provide comfort, as opposed to earning money to provide for the family.

Residing in the United States did not exclude Rangina's family, the Hamidis, from adhering to the Pashtun code of hospitality. Rangina shared the following story that while

40

A woman prepares to leave her courtyard to go out on the street dressed in an all-covering garment called a chaderi. Due to the conservative culture in Kandahar, women past puberty often do not go out on the street at all, but when they do, they wear chaderis or burqas to completely cover themselves. After the fall of the Taliban, this woman was able to attend university classes in Kandahar, but was required to wear this garment in the classroom and at all times on campus.

The palette of Kandahar burqas today is soft and muted. These modern burqas are fashioned from polyester, which holds the tight pleats that are considered proper.

she was in high school she was working on a project for one of her classes when family friends arrived unexpectedly. As was the custom, she and her sisters had to stop what they were doing and prepare and serve tea and food for the guests. When Rangina's father noticed that her face displayed a lack of interest in the guests, he immediately scolded her for not being a good Pashtun. As a hospitable Pashtun, hosts should never signal to guests that they are unwelcome or that their arrival has caused any inconvenience. Even a simple act of looking displeased is regarded as not being a good Pashtun. Presence in the United States did not change adhering to this code of hospitality for the Hamidis, a Pashtun family.

Nanawatay, seeking forgiveness or asylum, seems closely related to Melma palana. Nanawatay describes protection extended to a person who goes to an enemy and asks for forgiveness through some form of ritual humiliation; in return he will be given unconditional sanctuary. The cost to that person is loss of pride.

In one case, an eighteen-year-old boy was caught stealing from a family friend's home in their village. The boy's father feared that his friend might turn his son in to the police for justice. As an elderly father of ten daughters and only one son, the father gathered all of the village elders and asked them to accompany him to visit his friend's home and ask for forgiveness for his son's action. He took with him his son, the village elders, and a sheep and other food items as humble sacrifice for his son's bad deed. Along with the community elders, the father begged his friend, and in respect for the community's elders, the family friend forgave the son.

Nang is protection of the weak, and *Namus* is protection of women and country. A Pashtun tribesman must always ensure that his honor, and the honor of his countrymen, family, and women, is upheld. Pashtuns are extremely sensitive about the honor of any Afghan woman, and even a slight molestation of a woman is considered a serious and an intolerable offense. Cases of adultery and illicit relations are punishable by death with no mercy given to culprits, either male or female. For a man and his family, namus means sexual integrity and chastity of women in the household. The man must protect and defend his namus (the women of his immediate and extended family, the women of his village and community, and the women of Afghanistan at large) against physical and verbal threats from outsiders.

As an example, a married couple was invited to the wife's family house for dinner, where they ended up spending the night. An unmarried sister of the husband also accompanied the couple. In the middle of the night, the husband spotted the brother of his wife going inside the room where his sister was sleeping. The husband went immediately to the room where his sister was sleeping and killed his brother-in-law on the spot by stabbing him several times. The husband was jailed and at the trial the judge pardoned him on the basis that he was protecting his namus against someone who was trying to potentially harm his sister (his namus). Even though the civil code of Afghanistan does not have pardoning on the basis of protecting namus, the cultural tradition does.

Similarly, according to the principle of *Hewaad*, which is simply a word meaning country, the country must be

It sounds contradictory that Pashtun women can be strong, given the many layers of social and physical boundaries that they must live within.

protected from invaders at all cost. Historically, honor associated with protection of country served as a strong motivation among Afghans to fight for protecting their land. Pashtuns are proud even today of the fact that they were able to defeat British colonial powers in the early 1900s and to defeat Russians in 1989 in protecting their land. During hard times, Afghans have and will put their tribal disputes aside for the protection of their country against invaders.

Ba'd, or Badal, is probably the most controversial of the Pashtunwali code, as it encompasses justice and revenge against a wrongdoer. Wrongdoing can range from issuing an insult to committing murder and can lead to blood feuds that last for generations. While ba'd is usually settled between men, sometimes it involves exchanging a woman for a negative action. In the extreme case of an intentional murder, for instance, the Jirga (Council of Elders) of the community might solve the feud between the two families by exchanging the daughter, sister, or other female relative of the murderer as a bride for a son, brother, or cousin from the family of the one who was murdered. The intention behind this settlement is to bring harmony between the two families by joining the families in marriage. Of course, the reality may prove to be different.

Zhaba literally means tongue; in Pashtunwali, zhaba is a promise. True Pashtuns treat their word as the law by which they must live. A verbal promise is as strong as, and sometimes even stronger than, a written contract or notice.

Together, these and other Pashtunwali principles govern interpersonal and intertribal relationships. Not observing these customary laws is considered disgraceful and may lead to social punishments, such as expulsion of an individual or a whole family from the community or other harsh punishment, such as death. Among the Pashtuns, the dishonor of expulsion is regarded as every bit as bad as or even worse than physical death.

BOUNDARIES IN PATRIARCHAL SOCIETY

Pashtun societies are patriarchal. While Pashtunwali codes of conduct are designed for both men and women, the weight of decision-making is with the men. If a Pashtun man makes a decision about the affairs of his home and women that violates the codes of Pashtunwali, he will be labeled as *be-namus* (without integrity or honor). A Pashtun man with nang, or honor, will do everything and anything to save himself from being called be-namus, the strongest insult to an Afghan man. The easiest way to protect his honor is to protect his women. Measures are thus put in place to prevent women from taking even a small step to potentially dishonor their families. Hence, complete *parda* (veiling), publicly secluding women from men, barring women from serving in public life, or not allowing women to travel alone are ways to protect their women. All of these seclusions are understood as explicit ways to ensure women have no chance of jeopardizing their men's honor. The ultimate weight of honor lies on the shoulders of women. A small misstep or even the perception or appearance of impropriety can lead to dishonoring their families.

Physical and mental boundaries of a Pashtun woman are practical ways for keeping her from violating family honor. The physical boundaries emerge at puberty, when she begins to be limited to the family compound. She cannot leave without donning a full burqa and must be

Women are charged with rearing the sons of the household, but the balance of power between a male child and his mother shifts quickly as he grows up.

> *The easiest way to protect his honor is to protect his women. Measures are thus put in place to prevent women from taking even a small step to potentially dishonor their families.*

accompanied by a male or a female family adult. The four walls surrounding her family's home become the physical barriers for her safety.

Household practices clearly support distinction of public and private lives for women. Women are constrained from appearing on the roofs of their homes because they risk visibility to neighbors and men passing on the street. A proper Pashtun girl never answers a knock on the compound door, lest a stranger in the street see her. Most Pashtun families hang a heavy curtain immediately inside the main door of their home. The curtain prevents people walking along the road from seeing into the home, should the door be left open by children.

Girls require protection, as they are viewed as weak and incapable of making sound choices or decisions on their own. Girls must seek permission for every aspect of their lives. A good Pashtun girl must do only what her family tells or asks her to do. She must accept every decision, not for the sake of her individual happiness or satisfaction, but for the sake of her family's and father's name and honor.

Rangina's paternal aunt provided an example of protecting family honor. Her widowed mother engaged her, without her will, to a man she disliked. Her older brother, Rangina's father (who had become an urban man in Kabul), reminded his sister that she could break this engagement even on the night of her wedding. Rangina's aunt responded, "A good Afghan girl does not ruin her father's name like this.... I will ruin my life, but not the name of my father!" She willingly sacrificed herself for the sake of protecting her family—in the aunt's case, the honor of her deceased father's name.

While it is the duty of women to ensure the namus of their fathers and family, guarding the honor of women becomes the duty and responsibility of every father, brother, husband, son, and other male kin. In Pashtun societies it is not appropriate for men to talk about the women of their household to other men. Women's names must not be shared in public. Reference to women, particularly wives, is made indirectly by men calling their wives "mother of my children" or "woman of my household." Not identifying women by their names is another way to keep women from the public sphere in Pashtun communities and retain their honor intact.

LANDAY: How Women Speak Out

Within the boundaries of their private lives, Pashtun women express themselves in ways that are otherwise banned for them in public. Pashtun women are largely illiterate; they must rely on vocal and visual forms of expression to convey their messages to society. The most vocal form of expression by Pashtun women is the landay—folk poetry composed and sung for centuries by women, either alone or in groups. Landay is rooted in a culture in which knowledge, family values, customs, and beliefs were traditionally shared orally, rather than through books or other forms of writing.

Landays are based on everyday events and common themes in Pashtun life. Landays remain uncorrupted by outside influence, as the knowledge and practice of landay poetry is handed down strictly through generations of Pashtun people. Landays capture the ridicule and sarcasm of the strong-willed, critical, and vocal side of women. Pashtun women are often viewed as resolutely committed

Pashtun men are committed to maintaining honor for themselves, their families, their country—and especially for their women.

Fresh bread, yogurt, vegetables and fruit are fundamental to Kandahar cuisine.

to their families and communities and totally obedient to cultural norms. Their bold expressions in landays reveal another side—a side in which they push back and criticize traditions and rules they resent.

A landay has only a few formal properties. In the Pashto language, each landay has twenty-two syllables— nine in the first line and thirteen in the second. Several landays translated into English include:

> *My body is fresh as henna leaf:*
> *green outside; inside, raw meat.*

> *Of water I can't even have a taste.*
> *My lover's name, written on my heart, will be erased.*

> *My love gave his life for our homeland.*
> *I'll sew his shroud with one strand of my hair.*

> *Separation, you set fire*
> *in the heart and home of every lover.*

Women voice a range of topics in their landays. Popular themes include love and honor, the spiritual and natural world, departures and separations, exile, reunions, legendary and historical events, and social tragedies. Because the author's name is not included with the two-line verse, women are ensured anonymity and given the opportunity to express their feelings, even about taboo subjects such as sexuality, desire for free will, and disobedience. Indirectly, under the disguise of anonymity, Pashtun women use landay to express and start conversations in their restricted society.

The women at Kandahar Treasure use their lunch and tea breaks to practice their use of landays, and they create new ones among themselves to reflect their daily work with needle and thread:

Do not call me too much.
Am busy making your embroidered yoke.

If you want to do Kandahari khamak,
you must embroider beautiful diamonds in it.

Pick up your needles and embroider
Make pretty shawls for Kandahari young men

A GLIMPSE OF CHANGE

Since 2001 and the fall of the Taliban, the world's focus on Afghan women has magnified. Yet after more than fifteen years of investment by international governments and the aid communities, many of the world's developmental critics believe that the situation of Afghan women has remained unchanged. The great majority of women in Afghanistan are still illiterate and without much experience of working outside of their homes. The society and government of Afghanistan have not invested in building sustainable mechanisms for women seeking a means for survival for themselves and their dependents, let alone advancement.

National and international media focus on the negative stories that Afghan women face daily. While there are many social ills in Afghanistan today, including rising corruption and a volatile insurgency, positive developments across Afghanistan receive far less media attention. These developments are changing the face of Afghanistan and its history on a daily basis. A few examples in the textile field are the work of Zarif Design, Saraa Design and Laman, initiatives based in Kabul. All of these private companies and more, with the leadership of strong and professional individuals, use the Afghan tradition of embroidery and weaving of textiles to produce contemporary attire for men and women. Likewise, Kandahar Treasure, as an agent for change, was founded on the premise that women's traditional skill of fine hand embroidery could be used to create a brand and provide income to women, empower them economically, and strengthen a network of artisans across Kandahar.

It might sound contradictory that there are strong Pashtun women, given the many layers of social and physical boundaries that they must live within. However, the very honor that binds them to boundaries can also liberate women in Pashtun societies, provided that they break these boundaries respectfully and strategically.

Afghan women are survivors. While Pashtun Afghan woman may be viewed as silent and oppressed, a careful look at history and current-day events illuminates the strength of women who are silently fighting to change their society.

AFGHAN ROLE MODELS:
Malalai of Maiwand, Shakoko Nagahani, and Sitara Achekzai

There is a misconception that Afghan women have not had heroines in their history and, as such, role models for change must be sought outside of Afghanistan. However, Afghanistan's history includes laudatory examples of women warriors, poets, educators, and politicians. Three stories illuminate how these strong women worked to change their communities, while also enhancing the status for women across Afghanistan.

Malalai of Maiwand is an epic Pashtun heroine of the second Afghan-Anglo war of the late nineteenth century, whose encouragement gave young warriors the strength to stand and fight back against the British. Her famous landay is the following to the Afghan warriors:

Young love! If you do not fall in the battle of Maiwand,
By God, someone is saving you as a symbol of shame!

In her native language of Pashto:
Ka pa maiwand ki shaheed na shway,
Khudai julalaya, be-nangi ta di sateena!

Malalai is remembered throughout Afghanistan to this day and her example of bravery and love for country is shared in many major national gatherings and writings. Malalai is said to have held the Afghan flag from the flag-bearer who fell as a result of a British bullet. She sang the following landay as she held the Afghan flag:

With a drop of my sweetheart's blood,
Shed in defense of the Motherland
Will I put a beauty spot on my forehead,
Such as would put to shame the rose in the garden.

Malalai was also shot dead in the battle, and today her name has become a very popular girl's name throughout Pashtun communities.

Shakoko Nagahani was an ordinary woman whose fate in the early 1950s was unkind to her. She lost her husband to a heart attack soon after having three children with him. Faced by custom and tradition that would force her next to marry her brother-in-law, Shakoko refused to acquiesce. Instead, with the help of her father, she ran away to Kabul where she raised her three children as a single mother. Her tailoring skills provided income to feed her children and educate them at school. After her children reached early adulthood, Shakoko returned to Kandahar and lived in her village of Nagahan in Arghandab district. People came to know her by the name of "Shakoko of Nagahan." Shakoko's popularity as a role model derived from her courage and will to do what she wanted. She made her own decisions after becoming widowed and used the income from her textiles skills to shape the future for her children. Her age and experience won her the ability to insert herself publicly into society. Although she belonged to a powerful tribe of the King and had close relations to the King's family, there were many other women with these same connections who never used their power to better the lives of Afghan women.

Shakoko is remembered as riding alone on a horse as a means of transportation in her village. She rode without the full veil that women were expected to observe. More importantly, she forced the Jirga of her community to include her in their deliberations and to ensure her presence for all cases that involved women. No decision could be made about women without her input and insight. Over time, Shakoko became a role model, respected for her bravery, conviction, and commitment to her word.

Pashtunwali allowed her space for leadership in her community, even in the midst of codes that seemed extremely unfriendly to women. Although Pashtunwali has clear boundaries for women, those women wanting to maneuver within these boundaries in a respectful manner and without bringing shame to their society are not only respected but supported, even by the men in those same societies. Shakoko was highly respected in the 1950s and 1960s within her very conservative and traditional society

There is a misconception that Afghan women have not had heroines. However, Afghanistan's history includes laudatory examples of women warriors, poets, educators, and politicians.

Sitara Achekzai was a shining example of a woman who was strong and influential while being respectful of her culture. She served as one of only four women on the Afghan Provincial Council; her assassination was widely mourned.

as she worked to seek justice and fairness for women because she had built trust among her community and had the support of her family behind her to enable her to be an agent of change.

The outcome for Sitara Achekzai is not as fortunate. Sitara was born and raised in Kandahar, finishing twelfth grade at the Zaarghona Anna High School, the first girls' high school in Kandahar Province. Today, the school still graduates the largest number of girls in Kandahar city. She described herself as a "rebel," always questioning her father's and family's decisions and not following rules expected of good Kandahari girls. Sitara rode her bicycle to and from school each day in the 1970s. She recalled, "No one bothered me on the streets then."

While in twelfth grade, Sitara and her classmates learned that the twelfth grade boys from Kandahar were planning their annual field trip across Afghanistan. This opportunity was not afforded to girls. Sitara led a group of her classmates to visit the Department of Education of Kandahar and advocate for a similar trip for girls. After many hours of deliberation, the girls finally convinced the Director of Education to allow the girls to go on a trip similar to that of the boys. The only difference was that the girls could only go to the neighboring province of Helmand for a few days, while the boys traveled to five provinces throughout the country. Sitara and her classmates' next task was to convince their families. Their pleas were successful, and they all traveled to Helmand and enjoyed their time as young twelfth-graders in Kandahar in the 1970s.

Like millions of Afghans, Sitara and her family were eventually forced to migrate as a result of the Russian invasion. After twenty years of living in exile in Germany, Sitara and her husband returned from Germany to serve their country of birth. As an educated and passionate Pashtun woman who was working for change, Sitara became one of four female members elected to the Kandahar Provincial Council in 2006. Unfortunately, her dream of changing life for women in Kandahar was short-lived when insurgents assassinated her in front of her home in 2009. This cowardly act would not be sanctioned by Pashtunwali. The assassination of Sitara is an example of how times have changed, and this case is evidence that Pashtunwali's influence may be declining in a strong Pashtun society.

After the murder of Sitara, and numerous other women in Kandahar since the beginning of the twenty-first century, women are extremely fearful about their safety on the streets. Throughout Afghanistan, the rise in insurgency since 2006 has eliminated powerful tribal elders who upheld traditional values of peace, stability, and Pashtunwali. The collapse of the power structure within traditional Afghan society and the presence of guns and corruption among power brokers are greatly responsible for diminishing the codes and values of Pashtunwali. Some political leaders use Pashtunwali as a tool to gain advantage for themselves and their tribesmen over others without upholding to the core values of the Pashtun code.

Pashtun women's efforts to redefine the boundaries of their lives in Kandahar is no easy task. But times are changing, and so is the narrative for women. As the women of Kandahar Treasure embroider today, they still stitch within their strictly defined boundaries. Yet they are giving a new meaning to their stitches—the value of pride, ownership, and revival of a historic tradition. They are assuming roles as income providers in their homes, and in doing so, gaining new respect from family members. Pashtun women are carefully creating a network of artisans in a region where they have never had an opportunity to collaborate and work together. Exposure to women from differing tribes, villages, and backgrounds is paving the road for redefining boundaries for themselves and their daughters. There is hope that a new generation of Malalais, Shakokos, and Sitaras will rise in Kandahar and give life to the continuing struggle for justice and change that will respectfully broaden and redefine boundaries in women's lives.

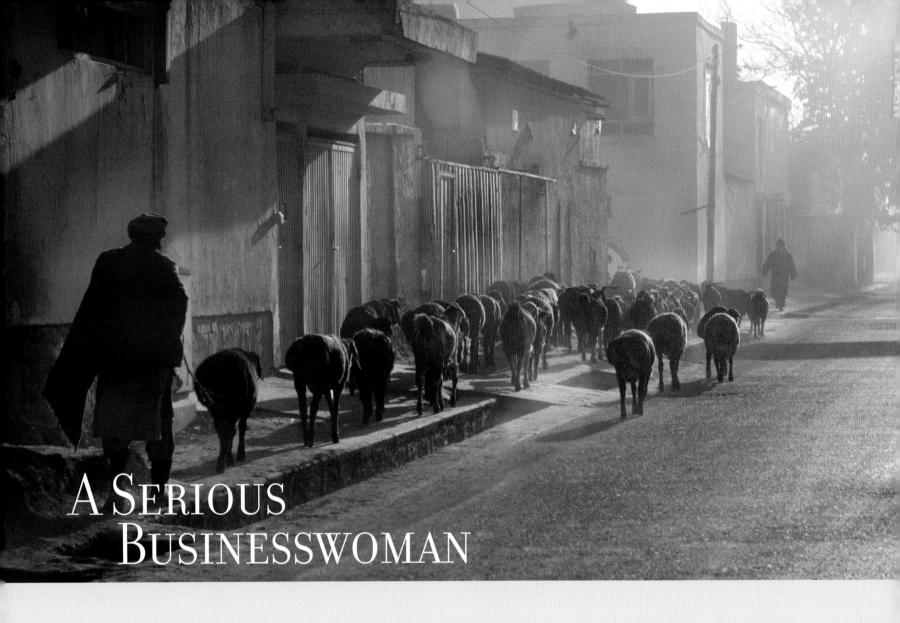

A SERIOUS BUSINESSWOMAN

NOORYA'S TALE

Afghan widows who lack re-sources to feed their families often turn to begging as a last resort. Noorya, a thirty-eight-year-old businesswoman, explains how begging catalyzed her resolve for change as a young widow.

What accounts for my bravery in doing this? It's need that forces you to do things. I had seven kids, *seven mouths to feed. No husband to do that. Begging people to give me food, flour, they would do it once or twice, but the third time they weren't going to give to me. I had to put my life in my palm—being exposed to danger, knowingly, because I had to feed my children. I didn't want to lead a life without integrity. I was scared initially. It was*

Even if wearing the burqa, being a woman alone in public in Kandahar is a risk. Widows with no male relative to accompany them to the marketplace must be exceptionally demure.

hard, but once I stepped out and started doing, after awhile I got used to it and now it's a part of my life and I'm not scared.

Khamak provided Noorya's lifeline to her future. She was a very young girl when she learned the skill; she quickly became expert at embroidering yokes for her brothers' shirts. By her mid-twenties, Noorya had established a home-based workshop in Kandahar, with khamak-embroidered men's yokes to be sold across the border in Pakistan.

Noorya organizes her business around a group of thirty-five women commissioners who take fabric for distribution to villages around Kandahar. Village embroiderers receive between 3000 and 8000 afghanis (about $45 to $119 US, depending on the neckline style) for completed work of the quality that Noorya expects. Noorya pays commissioners 100 afghanis (about $1.50 US) for each completed yoke. Noorya then takes the finished pieces to Pakistan where, after her expenses for fabric, supplies, and travel are subtracted, she nets around $45 per yoke. In addition to her village-based business, Noorya occasionally brings khamak items to Kandahar Treasure to sell on her behalf. Rather than going door to door, Noorya prefers that she can bring items to one place.

Over time, Noorya adopted business strategies to maintain consistent quality and to meet changing customer demand. To ensure that the village women return yokes on Noorya's fabric, rather than substituting a lower-quality material, she marks each piece with a symbol. She then matches symbols on completed yokes with the fabric sample at the workshop. Noorya's major selling season occurs during Ramadan, the Islamic holy month of fasting that rotates each year following the lunar calendar. As Afghans prepare for Eid, the culminating festival of celebration, all family members require new clothing. In anticipation of upcom-

Streets in Afghanistan cities and over the border in Pakistan have suffered from decades of armed conflict.

ing Eid festivals that fell during the hotter months of 2015 and 2016, she invested in rayon fabric for cooler garments. Her Pakistan vendors had shared that local men preferred wearing the lighter rayon as compared to the denser polyester fabrics of the past.

Noorya's trips to Pakistan, often three times in the month during Ramadan, require stamina and leave her exhausted. She chooses to ride in the back of a hatchback car on the journey between Kandahar and the border. Sitting in the more comfortable front seats costs 300 afghanis (about $4 US) more each way and "Why waste that money?" Crossing the final border into Pakistan involves walking a considerable distance on foot, as cars cannot pass through. Once in Pakistan, she hires a rickshaw and pays a man with a handcart to transport her goods.

Some Pakistani shopkeepers pay her directly for the goods; other merchants choose to consign the khamak yokes. An occasional vendor might question owing her money from his sales of her commissioned khamak yokes that she left from a previous visit. Noorya says there is nothing she can do about the delinquent merchants, but she is waiting for the afterlife. "If they are eating the earnings of my hard work now, there will be a day when they will have to answer."

Across the years, Noorya has learned to conduct business in ways that do not draw attention to her leaving home for conducting business. She credits a good sense of timing for her actions. When traveling to Pakistan, she departs early in the morning. Men have not yet come out of the mosque from morning prayers and begun sitting together on benches where they could observe her passing by. She returns at nightfall, when it is dark and the men are back in their compounds. When traveling, Noorya always dons old burqas so she will fit in when walking through the bazaars. She comments, "When I go out and I don't have it [burqa] on, I feel like I will die. We are so used to it. In the hot summer I feel like throwing it off. But that is a sin to show your face." Noorya also notes that now that her three sons are grown, "having them as men in the house keeps people from talking."

Having a steady income stream for the household allows Noorya to purchase daily needs of flour, oil, and sugar in bulk when she is in Pakistan. In the past, with a meager and unreliable income, she was forced to purchase these goods (imported from Pakistan) in small amounts and at higher prices in Afghan markets. Another expense awaits on the horizon. "In the coming time, I will have to find brides for my three grown sons and it will happen through khamak." A bride price of $10,000 US paid by the groom to the bride's family is common, plus the cost of the wedding.

Noorya concludes, "If it wasn't for khamak, I wouldn't be where I am today. I've been through days when my kids were young and they would see other kids eating bananas and I didn't have the money to buy bananas for them. To the point, one day I had gone somewhere and I didn't have the 10 afghanis to give to the driver to come back. I will never forget that day. I am very grateful that my life has changed and it's all because of khamak." Noorya says that in all this time, "I never had a twig come my way to stop me." She believes that going out of her home wearing an old ragged burqa and well-worn shoes symbolizes to the community that she is a serious businesswoman.

THREE

KHAMAK *in the* LIVES *of* AFGHAN FAMILIES

When we are born we are very naked and loud. The first thing we need is that we need to be wrapped up… we are born with just our skin and we need a second skin. Through our lives we need many, many other skins… we need protection, we need warmth… textiles are the first things that we touch and it's the first thing that touches us deeply.

Peter Sellars, Textile Society of America Symposium, 2014

Peter Sellars inspired Rangina to look at khamak embroidery with a new lens during his keynote address at the 2014 Symposium of the Textile Society of America. In his presentation, Mr. Sellars, a professor in the Department of World Arts and Cultures at the University of California, Los Angeles, celebrated textiles as embodying a rich panorama of human aspiration. He shared how textiles express a people's values, their priorities, and what they care about in life. For Rangina, Mr. Sellars's discussion enriched her understanding and interpretation of Afghan women's motivations for embroidering their textiles and the strength that ensues from their intimate interactions with cloth.

CLOTHING THE FAMILY

An Afghan newborn child is immediately wrapped in a khamak-embroidered cloth; the bundle is tightened with a khamak-embellished strap. The baby's head is partially covered in a soft cotton scarf, and the enveloped child is placed on a khamak-embroidered mat. Swaddling is intended to calm the baby and to aid in its sleep by preventing random arm and leg movement. All of the requisite textiles must be provided for the baby by the maternal grandmother prior to the baby's birth. Typically, the grandmother, aunts, and new mom's cousins embroider the layette. However, this traditional expression of love

The three guards who watch after Kandahar Treasure are valued by the women who work there for their dedication and cheerful nature. And of course, they always wear the finest khamak.

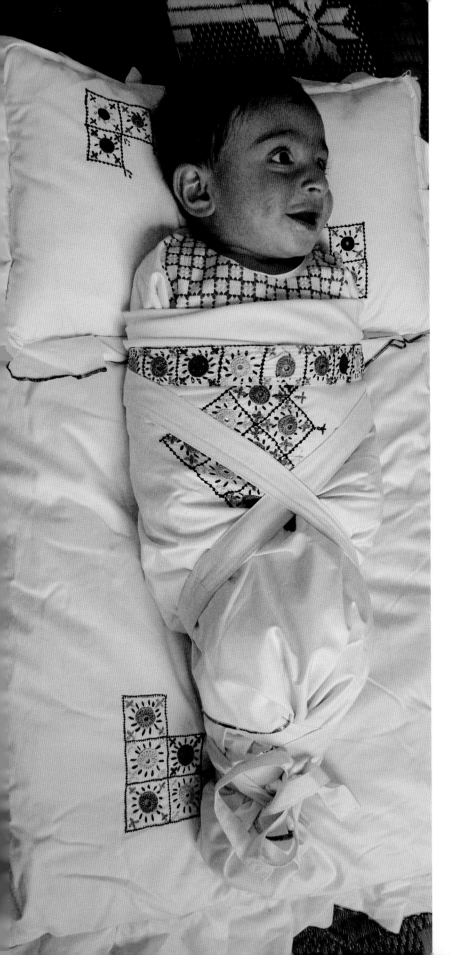

has become commercialized in recent years; many busy grandmothers commission the layette for completion by women outside the family. However, the gesture remains the same: the baby must be welcomed to the world in fine hand-embroidered textiles presented by the maternal grandmother. In wealthier families, a layette is provided for each new baby. Poorer families commonly stop providing new layettes after the first two children.

Textiles embellished with khamak embroidery follow Kandahar residents from birth to death. Both genders are adorned with khamak embroidery during childhood. Young girls are taught to embroider starting at around age six or seven. However, girls have little opportunity to wear the art themselves; boys become the main exhibitors of the fine needlework on tunics embroidered by their sisters or mothers.

In a culture where communication is often indirect, women's love for their brothers, sons, fathers, uncles, and other men in their family is conveyed nonverbally in the thousands of fine stitches on the men's tunics. As girls age, they will embroider "khamaki" tunics for their fathers or brothers before marriage and then for their husbands or sons after marriage. These fine stitches will remind the wearers of the women's love and dedication in making the tunics for them. As Mr. Sellars noted, textiles surrounding a loved one will not fade away as emotions and circumstances do. In many cases, the embroidered textile piece will outlast the lifespan of the individuals who produced and wore the textiles.

Not surprisingly, with emphasis on men's tunics, embroidery styles intersect with fashion. Three main styles are *shabazi* (a narrow strip of embroidery around the neck and down the right side of the chest), *patnusi* (a large rectangular shape of embroidery covering much of the chest), and *kamana* (a square over the chest narrowing to a V-shape at the bottom). Shabazi requires the least amount of work, and patnusi, the most. Kamana is the most popular style. Since 2003, Kandahar Treasure women have witnessed the revival of patnusi over shabazi. By 2015, shabazi nearly disappeared from the local market. Women

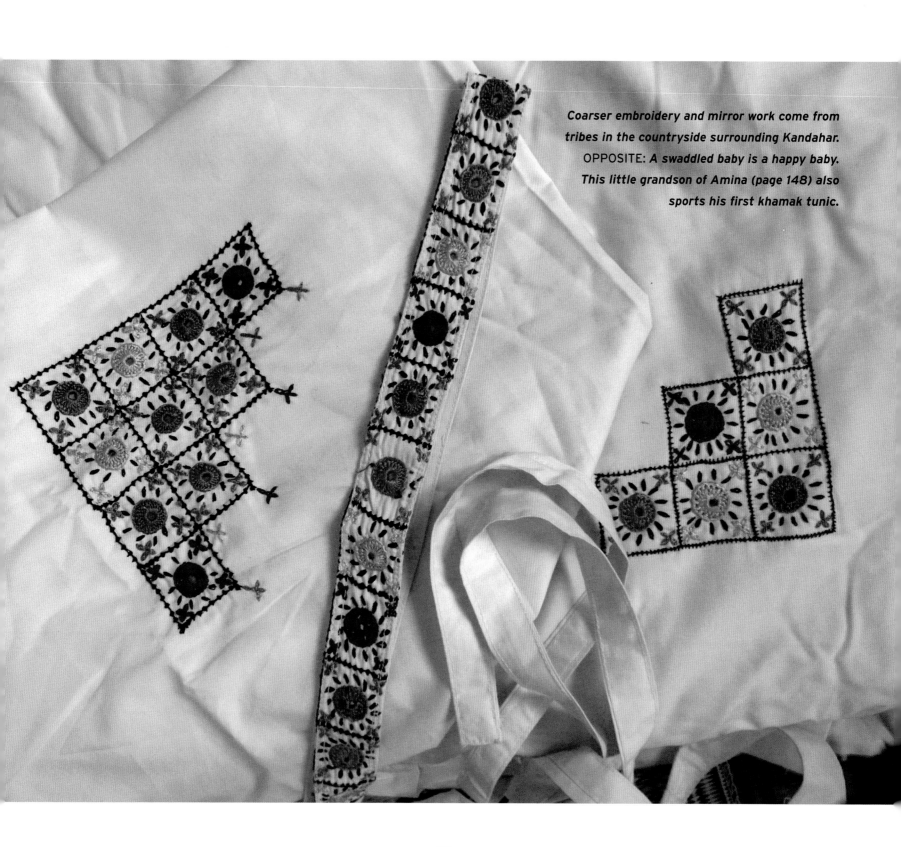

Coarser embroidery and mirror work come from tribes in the countryside surrounding Kandahar. OPPOSITE: *A swaddled baby is a happy baby. This little grandson of Amina (page 148) also sports his first khamak tunic.*

This newer style of embroidered tunic uses less khamak than the traditional style and thus is quicker to produce and more affordable.
OPPOSITE: The manager of one of the Kandahar Treasure shops wears a splendid example of traditional khamak.

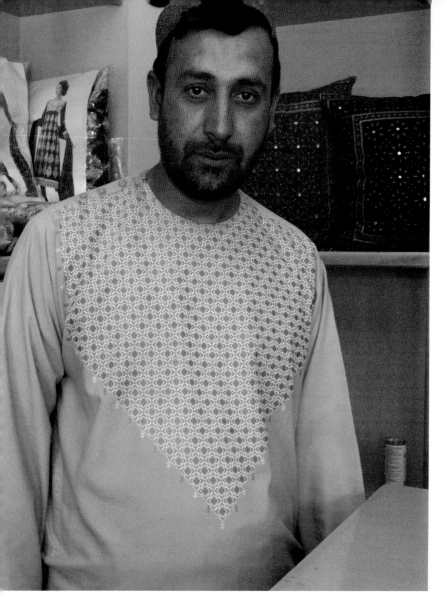

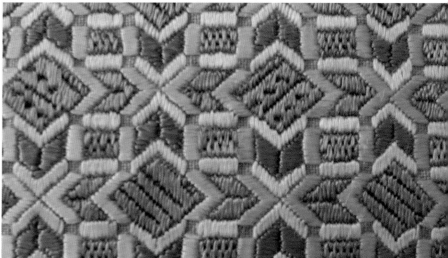

In a culture where communication is often indirect, women's love for their brothers, sons, fathers, uncles, and other men in their family is conveyed nonverbally in the thousands of fine stitches on the men's tunics.

only made this style as cheaper and quicker gifts for men not close to them.

Afghans sometimes have criticized women for focusing too much attention on adorning the clothes of their men and not creating khamak-embroidered clothing for themselves. Women have responded that their own clothes become dirty and damaged with daily chores. Instead they choose to adorn their homes with khamak-embroidered textiles. Women's space in Kandahar is the home—the compound bounded by the four walls surrounding them. This sacrosanct space is where the honor of the Pashtun culture lies and, by adorning this space, women express

their love for their homes and families. As interpreted from Sellars's perspective, women adorn spaces they care about and value.

MARRIED LIFE

In preparing for marriage in Kandahar, a girl must assemble a bridal trousseau consisting of items she will use in the home of her new extended family. The traditional Afghan home has a courtyard surrounded by rooms allocated to various family members. A bride entering her

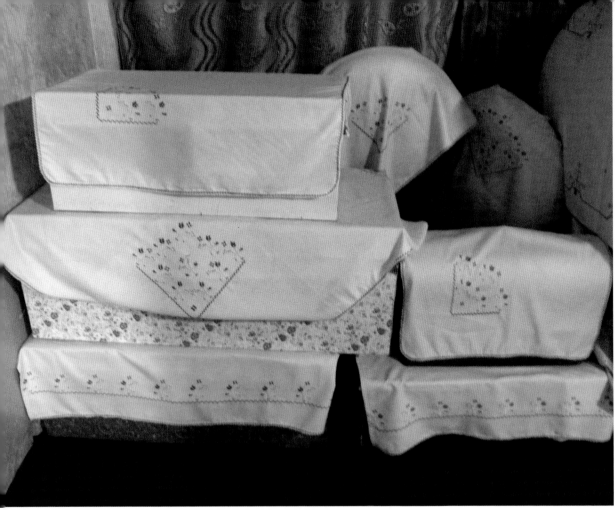
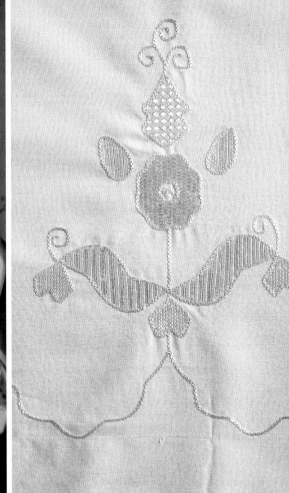

husband's home is offered one bedroom and, if lucky, a bathroom attached to that room. Only new daughters-in-law are allocated a special room in their in-laws' homes. Sisters of the house usually share one room with their mother until they marry and leave their natal home.

A bride embroiders all of the items for her new room. Before the introduction of beds and standing wardrobes, the bridal trousseau consisted of mattress covers for the floor, pillow covers, at least two large hangings to cover clothes hung on the wall, a burqa cover, a Quran cover, a coat cover for the husband's coat, a cloth used as a bib for the husband while shaving or trimming his beard, suitcase covers of rectangular cloths to cover multiple storage cases stacked at one side of the room for clothing storage, a door mat, and a large tablecloth to spread on the floor for eating.

With the introduction of beds and standing wardrobes, the bridal trousseau has evolved as well. Today, it likely consists of a bedspread with pillow covers and small heavily-embroidered decorative pillows, cloths to cover tables and televisions, table runners, and embroidered napkins to decorate the sofa. Large square napkins are embroidered for folding clothing into bundles before placing them in wardrobes. Embroidered suitcase covers are no longer needed, as the wardrobe has replaced multiple suitcases for storage of clothing.

Traditionally, a good Kandahari girl hand-embroidered the household items she took to her new home. Her allotted room in her husband's house—her very first room of her own—would be adorned and readied for her new life on the day of her marriage. Her in-laws and extended family would observe her work on display for the first time and appraise her workmanship. On the day after her wedding, the bride's mother and family customarily visits her in her new home. At this time, the mother shows the entire trousseau to the female-only gathering. The wom-

Fine embroidery finds its way onto all kinds of household textiles, such as storage case covers, wall hangings, and tablecloths.

It's not unusual for khamak embroidery to have as many as 70 stitches per inch, and to cover the base fabric entirely. The shawl opposite also has intricate drawn-work edgings.

The time, intensity of focus, and patience they learn while embroidering will help them endure the many hardships demanded of them in their fathers' households and later, their husbands' families.

Burqas today are often factory-produced with machine embroidery. These two older examples are entirely hand-worked in silk.

en watch with rapt attention to the range of items in the trousseau and also eagerly pass around the embroidered pieces for inspection. Some women will gain inspiration from new khamak designs in the trousseau, while others will evaluate and comment on the quality of the khamak workmanship.

Peter Sellars described how many cultures create textiles as "garments of praise." These garments shine and shimmer in their color, delicacy, and power. In applying Sellars's description to the bride's trousseau, these carefully and lovingly embroidered textiles embody his interpretation of "praise." The time devoted to producing such fine pieces requires the bride's intense concentration, patience, and meditation. The meditated stitches aid the embroiderer's internal growth and become permanent evidence of deep self-evolution. A good Pashtun woman dedicates her life to her family and to Allah. In Pashtun culture, her role is defined within the boundaries of her home. What she does with this space is up to her to adorn and decorate as she wishes. Her devotion to making her living space beautiful—a form of praise—is expressed in her fine khamak stitches displayed around her home and used by her family.

Sellars stated that life is composed of patterns, and learning to recognize the patterns helps individuals identify and anticipate what is coming next in life. As applied to khamak, learning a repertoire of embroidery patterns trains and prepares young women's minds for the rough road ahead of them and for the limited choices they will have as Pashtun women. The time, intensity of focus, and patience they learn while embroidering will help them endure the many hardships demanded of them in their fathers' households and later, their husbands' families. Advice given to young girls as they are marrying in a Pashtun family is to be a "bridge" in life. In order to sustain all forms of weight and burdens, a bridge must have a strong foundation. A strong Pashtun woman uses her strength of patience as her foundation.

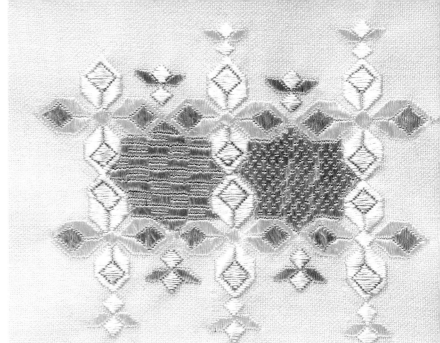

TEXTILES IN LATER LIFE

Embroidered textiles continue to play an important role in the life of a woman as she grows older. As she delves into married life and busies herself with bearing and rearing an average of six infants, she is showered with embroidered goods for her children. She must raise her daughters to learn the art of khamak and dress her sons with embellished tunics throughout their lives. As a woman ages, khamak-embroidered garments begin to appear in her personal wardrobe. A mature Kandahari woman will start wearing classic, white-on-white embroidered pants under a dress of any color and fabric. If she can afford it, she will also embroider a pure silk, white-on-white scarf to complete her ensemble. When she is no longer able to embroider due to poor eyesight, her loved ones—daughters, daughters-in-law, or even granddaughters—will provide her with khamak-embroidered clothing. Or, the woman may commission garments for completion by embroiderers outside the home. An older respected woman in Kandahar will wear her white-on-white embroidered pants and head scarves until she dies.

When she is no longer able to embroider due to poor eyesight, her loved ones—daughters, daughters-in-law, or even granddaughters—will provide her with khamak-embroidered clothing.

In contrast, a Kandahari man will wear embroidered tunics from the day he is born mostly until he becomes a grandfather, at which time he will cease to wear embroidered clothing. As an elder he will wear a plain tunic and pants to exhibit his respect and dignity in the community. Afghan men live very serious lives, and a serious man cannot don embellished attire at an old age. The reverse is true for women.

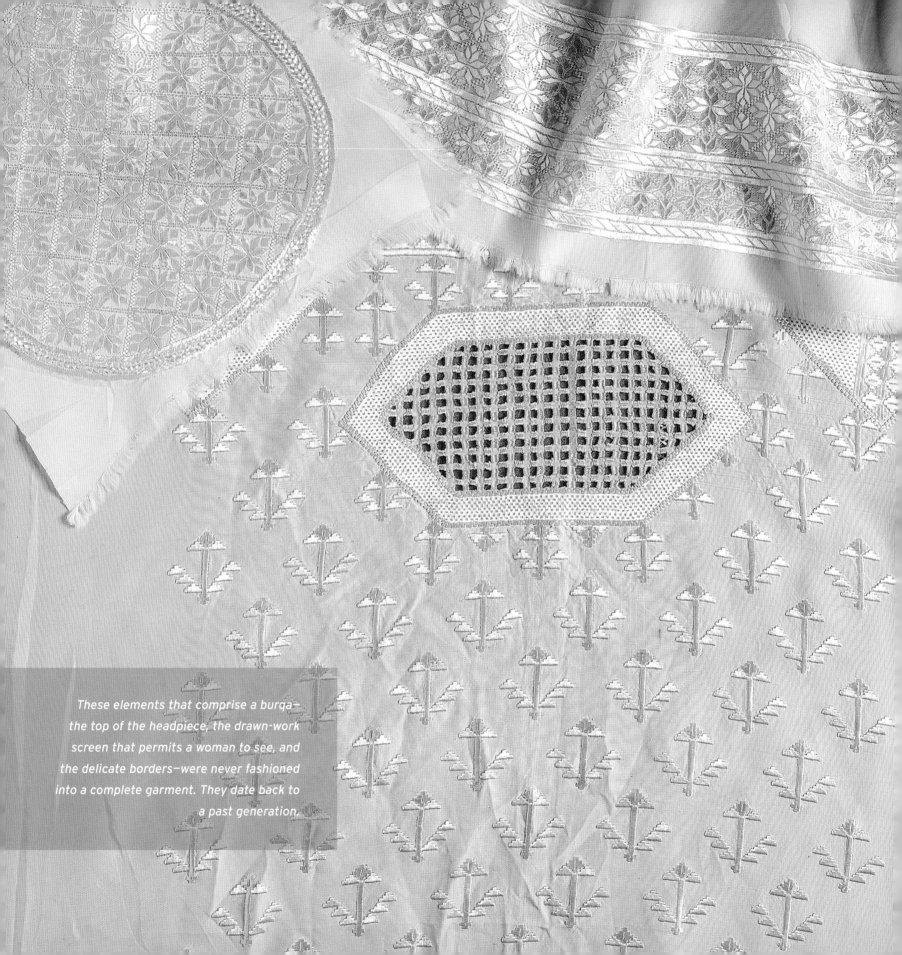

These elements that comprise a burqa—the top of the headpiece, the drawn-work screen that permits a woman to see, and the delicate borders—were never fashioned into a complete garment. They date back to a past generation.

*In more modest homes,
the hangings are often
done according to
free-form patterns
and with larger stitches.*

AFGHANS IN THE DIASPORA

As Rangina left a business meeting in New York City, she spotted a fresh-fruit stand across the street. Hungry, she walked to the stand and asked for bananas. As the seller gave her the fruit she handed him payment. However, the man refused the money and replied with a smile, "I can afford to treat my Afghan sister." Surprised, Rangina asked, "How do you know I am an Afghan?" He replied, "Who else wears white khamaki pants!" Rangina looked down to her embroidered pants and smiled.

The decades of war in Afghanistan have dispersed Afghans to adopted communities throughout the world. Afghans joke among themselves that there is no country in the world today without Afghans in it! Afghans immigrating to the United States have settled primarily in the Washington D.C., metro area, New York, Chicago, Atlanta, Boston, and the San Francisco and Los Angeles areas of California. Like other refugee communities throughout the world, Afghans have retained their culture through language, food, music—and dress, the most visible form of cultural preservation.

For Afghans living in the diaspora, khamak has become a symbol of recognition and pride. Any man or woman wearing garments with khamak embroidery is recognized immediately as an Afghan by other Afghans. Immigrants' love for and use of traditional Afghan attire has increased in recent years within Afghan communities on foreign soil. Since 2002, many Afghans in the diaspora have been able to return to their country of birth either for short visits or work opportunities. These visits have allowed them to reconnect with their culture and purchase goods, including Afghan-style clothing, which may not be readily available outside of the country.

To show allegiance to their heritage, Afghans in the United States proudly wear traditional Afghan attire to weddings, public ceremonies, annual picnics, and national soccer tournaments held among Afghan communities throughout the country. One young Afghan-American teenager, born and raised in America and who has never

For Afghans living in the diaspora, khamak has become a symbol of recognition and pride.

traveled to Afghanistan, stated, "Wearing Afghan-embroidered clothes is my only way to physically express my desire to get to know my heritage."

Likewise, residents of Afghanistan exhibit their national allegiance when traveling outside the country. A young development aid worker in Kandahar said that he proudly wears his embroidered tunic when he leaves Kandahar to go to Kabul or even when traveling abroad. He explained that wearing his khamak-embroidered tunics when he is outside the country makes him feel more Afghan. The embroidered attire makes him feel connected to his home, to his family, and to his loved ones. He stated, "When I am lonely in my travels outside of my hometown of Kandahar, my embroidered clothes make me feel at home." Sellars noted that in these times of modern alienation, mass-produced products lack a unique identity connected with the wearer. In contrast, pride and pleasure can come with garments made with care and love for a specific person. By wearing his embroidered Afghan clothes, the development aid worker recognized the family's love and pride he carries with him.

In completing his keynote address, Sellars stated, "To create in a piece of work that you are actually touching—a vision you can live in and live with—makes you live differently and better." Women embroiderers of Kandahar are sharing their vision of beauty through their fine stitches. Afghans adorn their lives with embroidered artifacts. They wear the admiration of their loved ones; through khamak they exhibit self-respect as Afghans. Defining their identity with embroidered textiles within and outside of Afghanistan expresses honor and pride. As with many cultures in the world, the handwork of women disseminates that pride.

FOUR

The FAMILY'S JOURNEYS *to the* WEST *and* BACK

In the compounds, people spent their time with the group.
As far as I can tell, none of my Afghan relatives
was ever alone or wanted to be.

Tamin Ansary, *West of Kabul, East of New York*

Rangina Hamidi entered the world with high expectations placed on her tiny shoulders. Initially, family members expressed disappointment. After three daughters, her parents hoped their fourth child would be a boy. Her grandmother, grieving from the death of a teenage son to cancer, intensified the anticipation. She yearned for her daughter-in-law's next child, a son, to help to soothe the loss of her own child. Amidst the unhappiness, Rangina's grandfather confronted the family. "What do you mean, it's not a boy? Of course we're happy it's a girl." To reinforce his assertion, the grandfather announced the birth by sending cookies and sweets to other homes in the community. Some neighbors asked why he was sending sweets if the new baby was a girl. He responded, "She is no less than a son to us."

At her naming ceremony, Rangina's grandfather further amplified his granddaughter's importance, "She is going to grow up to be someone very special. She will make the whole family very proud." Today, Rangina continues to feel the weight of her grandfather's expectations, "Growing up, I always heard what my grandfather said. It guided me as the family's expectation for me."

The streets of Kandahar have suffered much damage since this photograph was taken in 2009, but efforts are constantly underway to repair and rebuild.

When this photograph was taken in 2006, girls had more opportunity to attend school and to move freely in their community.

Respect for education filtered back several generations in Rangina's family. Her paternal grandfather insisted his sons and daughters attend the village school. Neither grandparent was educated. The village residents ridiculed his actions; they didn't share his ambition that village children receive an education. So eager for learning, the grandfather even tried out school as an adult, but his brothers made so much fun of him that he stopped attending.

Ghulam Haider Hamidi, Rangina's father, completed a degree in education at the University of Kabul. In doing so, he fulfilled his father's dream he would pursue a teaching career. However, his love did not reside in teaching; work in finance and accounting held greater pull. Upon completing university education, Mr. Hamidi worked hard to progress from his provincial position in Kandahar to a national appointment in the Ministry of Finance. By the time Rangina was a year old, the family had moved to a new life in Kabul.

During his first few years in the Ministry, Mr. Hamidi balanced previously unsolvable budget issues. Rangina said, "We were poor, but my father was a hard-working man, doing the best that he could for our family—by then composed of five daughters." Following the invasion of Afghanistan by the Russians in 1979, the Communists controlled the government. However, Mr. Hamidi refused to join the Communist party. As civil conflict escalated, he clandestinely worked against the government by passing anti-Communists information among ministry employees. Rangina said, "My father was not a physical fighter. He was supporting the mujahideen by distributing printed material. If he had been caught by the Communists, it would have cost him his life."

By 1981, the Finance Minister heard that Mr. Hamidi was taking part in dangerous underground activities. The Minister advised him to leave Afghanistan before he was targeted for assassination. He knew Mr. Hamidi was supporting a large family, all women. In his departing com-

In the early 1980s, it was illegal to flee Afghanistan. A family could not announce officially or even tell neighbors they were departing.

ments, the Minister confided that if they did not have the Communist regime, what Mr. Hamidi had done to solve national budget issues would have been greatly rewarded.

In the early 1980s, it was illegal to flee Afghanistan. A family could not announce officially or even tell neighbors they were departing. If spotted escaping by the Russians, their transportation would be bombed. To begin their flight, the Hamidis first returned to Kandahar, under the ruse of "visiting relatives for a month or so." Locating a truck and driver willing to take a large family to Pakistan proved challenging. As Mr. Hamidi's father was deceased, he was solely responsible for his extended family. The escape group included his wife, five daughters, his mother, one unmarried sister, and himself—nine Afghans in all.

Being a four-year-old child in 1981, Rangina remembered only a few impressions of Afghanistan. One imprint remained from the courtyard of the family's home in Kabul. Rangina was playing with her younger sister while their mother swept the courtyard. Rangina recalled seeing a black cloud overhead and wondered why it wasn't white as clouds were supposed to be. It was black residue floating in the air from a tank blown up by the mujahideen. On another occasion Rangina marveled at the pretty orange sparks in Kandahar's early evening sky—this time shell fire from armed conflict. Finally, Rangina relished an incident that occurred during her last day in Kandahar. Her father had taken her in the early morning to buy *jalebi* sweets. She remembers dancing back into the house, "I have jalebi. You don't have any!" She was not a meek child.

THE NEVER-ENDING NIGHT

The family members squashed together on benches in the open-backed truck as the family fled Afghanistan on a cold, moonlit night in February, 1981. Two guards escorted the escapees. Heavy blankets provided warmth to the women and children. Fearful of being spotted by Russians, the driver avoided the regular route from Kandahar to Quetta. Instead, he drove over rutted back roads as he negotiated across mountains and through villages on the ten-hour journey. Along the way they passed recurring evidence of armed conflict and indications that some escapees failed to reach the border. A bride's body hung from a burnt-out car near the road. The woman's henna-covered hands and rings offered shocking evidence of her recent nuptials.

Fear and anxiety accompanied the Hamidi family throughout the long night. Suddenly nearing a mountain, the driver yelled, "Pray as hard as you can." He gunned the truck, tearing over the road. Later the driver explained he spied an airplane coming over the mountain. If they had been spotted, the truck would have been targeted for bombing. As dawn appeared on the horizon, the children awoke in Pakistan. Rangina's father climbed down from the truck, and with the driver and guards, broke ice to prepare ablutions for the first morning prayer. He stood alone crying as he departed his homeland.

When they crossed the border in 1981, Mr. Hamidi's five daughters were ages three, four, eight, eleven, and fifteen years. Two additional babies—both boys—were born to the family while living in Pakistan. Soon after their arrival, Mr. Hamidi began the process of application for the family's immigration to the United States. Initially, they settled in Chaman just inside the Pakistan border; however, an early incident created anxiety for Rangina's mother. As the two youngest daughters did not possess photos required for the application papers at the United Nations Refugee Agency, Mrs. Hamidi took them to be photographed. On the return home, a bearded man with a turban and kalashnikov confronted the mother and daughters, demanding they stop. The mujahed questioned whether they were Communists fleeing Afghanistan. The incident so frightened Mrs. Hamidi that she announced she was not staying in Chaman.

A PLEASANT NEIGHBORHOOD

The family departed for Quetta, where they settled into a life as refugees for the next seven years. Mr. Hamidi found employment as a clerk with a private Afghan business. After working for two years, he saved and borrowed sufficient funds to move the family from a rental property to a purchased home in a poor neighborhood on the outskirts of Quetta. As other Afghan families built homes, the area grew into a friendly community of poor families. Women visited during daytime hours, going from house to house wearing headscarves, but without burqas. Children played together safely on the street. Rangina says, "My childhood—I remember being very happy." Living in the pleasant neighborhood contrasted sharply with life in Afghan refugee camps set up elsewhere in the city.

Pakistan public schools denied attendance to Afghan children. With his limited salary, Mr. Hamidi could afford to send only Rangina and her younger sister to a private school. Rangina took pride in the sisters' progress in school, often out-performing their Pakistani classmates in the Urdu-based curriculum. The older sisters were pre-teens or teens. Going to school was not advisable for them in the Pakistani refugee environment. When a girl turned ten years old, the boundary walls of her home began to enclose her in the household. She started covering her head and no longer played outdoors.

By having a house in Quetta, the family hosted a revolving door of guests. Some visitors stayed for four to six months in the small, already crowded home. Pashtunwali tradition required extending hospitality to all who visited. Rangina recalled, "I grew up in a house full of people. Always!"

In Pakistan, there were few opportunities to buy readymade clothing. Rather, women purchased cloth in

Ghulam Haider Hamidi was a leader of great wisdom and integrity. His assassination in 2011, when he was Mayor of Kandahar, was devastating to his family and to his countrymen, and has given his daughter, Rangina, even greater resolve to help her country.

the market, which they sewed themselves or took to a tailor. Rangina's second oldest sister, a talented seamstress, capitalized on this entrepreneurial opportunity. Together with her older teenage sister, who machine-embroidered women's pants, and their mother, who sewed the hems and buttons, the trio soon operated a thriving tailoring business out of their home. During the last days of Ramadan and immediately before the Eid celebrations, the women rarely slept, as they had so many orders to complete.

DANGER FOR YOUNG GIRLS

In the mid-1980s, the Quetta neighborhood dynamics changed dramatically. A wealthy drug-dealer from Kandahar purchased a large plot of land and built a mansion at the end of the street—a street otherwise comprised of small plots and small houses. Men with long beards and big turbans arrived, slinging kalashnikovs at their sides. Street life suffered as the mujahideen stronghold took control. Women rarely visited their neighbors anymore, and only when wearing burqas. Children no longer played freely in the streets.

At the time, Rangina and her sister were the only children on the street attending school. One day in 1987, as the girls donned their uniforms and backpacks for school, a man knocked on the door. Mr. Hamidi answered, talked with the visitor, and then returned to tell the girls they would not be attending school that day. The visitor, a mujahed up the street, threatened Mr. Hamidi that if he didn't pull his daughters out of school, the girls might suffer drenching with acid poured over their bodies. A friend's daughter had already been severely scarred. Mr. Hamidi hoped to keep his daughters in school through sixth grade; however, the visit convinced the girls' parents that they should not take chances for their daughters' safety. Together with their father, the daughters returned to their third grade classroom and brought their schoolbooks home for the last time.

BECOMING THE HAMIDI FAMILY

The family acquired the surname *Hamidi* as a requisite for their immigration to the United States. In Afghanistan, surnames did not exist. Women were given a name at birth, but the name had little significance in society. Using a woman's name outside the household and in public brought dishonor on the family. Across their lives women acquired a series of nicknames within their natal households and as they married. Although Rangina was given her great-grandmother's name, Sabera, at birth, she could not be called Sabera, out of respect for her relative, who was still alive. Instead, an aunt nicknamed her Rangina.

In a tribal society, one's name links the person to others in the lineage. Outside the household, Rangina was known as Rangina, the daughter of Ghulam Haider. When it came time to immigrate and establish a surname, some Afghans chose names linked to their home village or provinces in Afghanistan, such as Nuristani, derived from a province named Nuristan, meaning "land of light." Rangina's family followed another common naming pattern, that of honoring an ancestor. Her great-grandfather's name was *Hamid*. Since the family followed in his lineage, they became *Hamidi*—the surname printed for the first time on their immigration application papers.

At the end of 1987, the Hamidi family learned of their approval for immigration to the United States. Exactly seven years since leaving Afghanistan, the Hamidis departed Pakistan on February 18, 1988. Rangina was eleven years old. Upon arrival in Virginia, the family began the settling-in process, with the children enrolling in various schools and Mr. Hamidi finding employment as an accountant. At first the Hamidi women felt lonely after a life of constantly hosting a household full of visitors. But later the sisters confided, "This is so much nicer. We don't have people coming and staying with us for months at a time. Cooking, cleaning, and caring for them was more than a full-time job."

BLENDING AFGHAN CULTURE
with a NEW LIFE IN THE U.S.

When asked about boundaries in her life, Rangina said, "I've never felt that I had boundaries. I've never felt that I've been controlled. There were values and customs that I followed because I felt they were right. Dating was a no-no. We didn't go to sleepovers at friends' homes. We didn't go to the cinema all through high school. We didn't ask for reasons; we just knew there were things we were not supposed to do. I knew the limits and I didn't cross them. At the same time I felt so much love in what our parents gave us. I saw so many other kids who didn't receive all the love and attention we did. My father never, ever treated me, or any of his daughters, as if we were less than boys. He loved his girls."

Islam remained central to the Hamidis' daily life in the United States. Rangina explained, "Growing up, we always knew that we were Muslim. That's an identity. I didn't know an extreme version of Islam. You prayed five times a day, you fasted during Ramadan, paid your charity, were nice to people, didn't steal—that's Islam." In elementary school, the Hamidi girls learned other cultural practices as well. For instance, in their first school days, an Afghan classmate helped Rangina and her sister take pepperoni off their pizza when it was served for school lunch. They didn't know what pepperoni was, nor that it was derived from pork. To ease the transition for the Hamidis and other Afghan families, retail stores began offering Halal meat and their much-loved Afghan bread—foods that helped sustain Afghan identity in their new country.

COLLEGE DAYS

At the University of Virginia, Rangina double-majored in Religious Studies and Women's Studies. During her college years, several pivotal events contributed to dramatic change in Rangina's life and served as first steps toward her eventual return to Afghanistan. After her sophomore year, she attended a Muslim conference in Washington, D.C. When she picked up her Muslim friend for the conference, his mother suggested that it would be wise if she covered her head. She gave Rangina a scarf, a *hijab*, and helped her tie it properly. At the end of the first days of the conference, Rangina removed the scarf when she got in the car to drive home. On the final day, she left the hijab on, wondering, "What would it feel like to wear a scarf all the time?"

When she returned, her parents said nothing. On the following Monday, she wore the scarf as she departed for her summer job, telling her parents that she was thinking about permanently covering her head in public. As she left, her father advised, "Do it only if you are serious about it." Rangina wanted to show, "I am not like any of the oppressed women in the books we were reading in Women's Studies classes." She continued, "Here in America wearing the hijab forced me to become public in who I am. I was a shy, timid girl before. I know that the hijab played a huge role in helping me to come from where I was to who I am currently. I think subconsciously I was preparing myself for where I am today."

As a Women's Studies major, Rangina yearned to learn, first-hand, about women's lives in Afghanistan. Her university advisor, an Iranian-American, urged her to return. By 1998, the Taliban were in power, controlling much of Afghanistan. Unable to return to Afghanistan, Rangina instead traveled to Pakistan for a three-week stay with a sister and aunt who remained among the Afghan community in Quetta. After ten years away, Rangina was the first woman in her family to travel back to where she had lived as a child.

Rangina recalled a particularly troubling event during her stay. She joined the women in a neighborhood house who were dressed to attend a wedding. Suddenly, the husband returned. He announced that he had invited ten guests for dinner and demanded that the women prepare the meal. The women removed their festive attire and started cooking. Rangina asked her sister if this was what life was like in Quetta. "I couldn't understand this world,

Refugee camps in Quetta provided safe haven for fleeing Afghans during the Soviet invasion.

Afghan streets at dusk on a chilly December day.

The women in a neighborhood house were dressed to attend a wedding. Suddenly, the husband returned. He announced that he had invited ten guests for dinner and demanded that the women prepare the meal. The women removed their festive attire and started cooking.

even though as an Afghan I was part of it. My father had never treated us this way."

While hoping to learn about women's lives, Rangina reflected, "I came back to the U.S. so disturbed and hurt, and more confused than when I went. What could I possibly do to help women? I had gone to write my thesis on women and the Taliban. But it was so much more complicated than just women and the Taliban. There were so many other issues—cultural issues. I was so young. I couldn't make sense out of what I had seen."

IMPACTS FROM 9/11

By fall 2000, Rangina had completed her university degree. After the September 11, 2001, attacks in the United States, the news media sought out Rangina as an articulate expert who was Afghan and wore the hijab. In response, her father urged, "Go to the place [Afghanistan] and experience what you are talking about. At least return to Pakistan." In December, she took a three-week vacation from her job at a non-profit agency in Virginia. With

an airline ticket provided by her father, Rangina returned once again to Pakistan, with a goal to learn about life in the Afghan refugee camps in Quetta.

Prior to departing, people heard about Rangina's trip and, in less than a week, she collected more than $10,000 in donations from family, friends, and random contributors. Rangina said,

I'm this little bank with $10,000. I have no contacts on the ground. I don't even know what development work is. In Pakistan I bought winter shawls, head scarves for women, Vaseline for skin moisture, socks for kids, coats, sweaters—as much winter stuff as I could buy—but there was still so much money left as these things were cheap there. So I'm giving out what I bought to random people, squatter communities living in tents, poor family friends who have escaped. At the end of the third week, I had given out all the goods and left the remaining $1,000 with my aunt.

I was coming home on the plane on January 1 of 2002. I sat thinking I had just wasted $10,000. I bought them sweaters, but the sweaters will grow old. The food has been eaten. What did this do to help the people? It didn't do anything to help. If I ever go back, I'm not giving cash. I'm going to do something with the women, building an infrastructure for them to build their own capacity.

On the return flight to the United States, Rangina recalled the thriving tailoring business her sisters and mother had operated in Quetta. She also remembered that some women did Afghan embroidery to earn money. Ideas brewed—embroidery, tailoring, something with textiles, a work-related entity that would help women. Rangina said, "So the idea for what eventually became Kandahar Treasure came into my head on my flight back to America in 2002."

Becoming an Independent Woman

Zia Jaan's Story

Zia Jaan initiated our afternoon conversation, "I don't see Kandahar Treasure as Kandahar Treasure. It's my home." Prior to joining Kandahar Treasure, Zia Jaan moved from household to household—from one miserable situation to another—always under the command of men. Now, at age forty-five, Zia Jaan relishes the freedom she feels each day among the courageous and independent Kandahar Treasure women with whom she works.

Zia Jaan's path to independence traversed through two heartbreaking marriages and an ever-widening web of familial enmeshment. At age eighteen, while visiting her sister in Pakistan, a brother-in-law arrived from Afghanistan and whisked her

Zia Jaan is a master tailor and an important part of the leadership team at Kandahar Treasure. For Rangina, she is part of the family.

home for an engagement party with a man she had never met. The couple wed three months later. Zia Jaan's first three years of happily-married life fell apart when a first and then a second co-wife joined the household—the second co-wife being Zia Jaan's sister-in-law from her own deceased brother.

Difficulties soon arose among the co-wives. Zia Jaan recalled an afternoon when she heard a clamor from people yelling and screaming outside her room. Her father stood in the courtyard demanding that the second co-wife, his daughter-in-law, turn over the children of his deceased son. As the grandfather, he was entitled to the children. Zia Jaan berated the co-wife, "If you cared so much about your children, you wouldn't have come and married my husband." Resentments among the co-wives escalated. Two days later, while Zia Jaan was drinking tea, her husband came into her room and announced, "You are a good wife, a good woman, but I don't need you anymore." A divorce soon followed. Zia Jaan pleaded with her husband to allow her two sons to remain with her. Her father even took the case to the community mosque for discussion. However, as the children's father, the

husband retained custody under Afghan law.

Devastated by her husband's abandonment and deprived of her children, Zia Jaan moved back to her elderly father's home. In Afghanistan, when a woman returns to her natal home, the community talks. The divorced or widowed woman feels miserable, as she is viewed as a burden on her family once again. Zia Jaan was no exception in her loneliness and pain.

Zia Jaan's father, concerned that he might die not knowing his daughter's future, reviewed numerous proposals for his daughter to marry again. Over and over, Zia Jaan refused, saying, "What good did I see from my first husband that I want to marry again?" Finally, she accepted marriage with a widower much older than herself and with a family of four sons and three daughters. Three years of "misery and pain" followed as she cared for her slowly dying husband. Her son from the second marriage barely knew his father. Following her husband's death, tradition required that she perform the *iddah*, a period of three months and ten days during which she was secluded at home to determine if she were pregnant. Had she been pregnant

and chosen to leave the household, the child would remain in the deceased father's home after its birth.

Today Zia Jaan remains in her second husband's household. This extended family includes her son from the second marriage, seven stepchildren, three of the stepsons' wives, and their numerous children. Among the stepdaughters and sisters-in-law, all remain at home throughout the day at their husbands' or brothers' requests. Only Zia Jaan leaves for work. When speaking of her stepchildren, Zia Jaan considers herself lucky, "They don't make me feel like I'm their stepmother. They constantly remind me that for them I'm both their mother and their father. They respect me, take care of me, and are kind to me. Comparing my life with the two co-wives I was sharing with my first husband, to now living with my stepsons and stepdaughters, I very much prefer this life to the first." As a widow going out from the household to Kandahar Treasure on a daily basis, Zia Jaan takes special care to behave in a way that would not lead to rumors about her actions or bring dishonor on the household.

When I asked Zia Jaan if she ever saw her first two sons after the

Zia Jaan and Rangina consider an outfit to wear to Zia Jaan's son's wedding. Weddings offer women an opportunity to dress up and celebrate in their separate "women's room."

divorce, her pained face provided an instant answer, "Only rarely. I try and try to this day, but it's very difficult to forget that I have two other children." Several years ago she did receive an invitation to her sixteen-year-old son's wedding. "Those three nights were the happiest moments of my life in a long time. Being with him and seeing him as a groom made me feel the happiness that I had in the first years of my married life. When I came back home, I'm constantly thinking about whether my sons will ever come back to me and accept me

as their mother." Zia Jaan fears that may never happen, as by marrying her son to the niece of his step-mom, the family will want to keep him under that family's influence and away from her.

In the course of her divorced and widowed lives, Zia Jaan taught herself to tailor garments as a means of contributing to the households. However, Zia Jaan and her tailoring expertise nearly eluded Kandahar Treasure. Ten years ago, Kandahar Treasure needed a new tailor for completing a large order. They identified a prospec-

tive tailor; however, she was not at home when a Kandahar Treasure staff member arrived. A member of the household knew of Zia Jaan's tailoring skills and recommended her to fulfill the urgent order. Zia Jaan completed the order in ten days, much to Kandahar Treasure's satisfaction. When asked to stay on at Kandahar Treasure, Zia Jaan received a mixed reception among her stepchildren. However, upon consulting family elders and receiving their permission, she agreed to continue her tailoring at Kandahar Treasure. As Kandahar Treasure grew, the tailoring room expanded from three tailors to five and now eight, all trained under Zia Jaan. She laughed, "Now they are at a level that they make fun of my work. They have gone above me and I'm happy for them. They recognize that I've been instrumental in their learning or improving their skills. I receive recognition from them."

When Zia Jaan first went out to work at Kandahar Treasure, despite receiving elders' permission, men in her household still harbored fear that she was going to find a boyfriend or have an affair. They took their time investigating what she was doing, even tracking her down. Occasionally, a family member still offers, "We will give you the money you are earning at Kandahar Treasure—stay home." Zia Jaan counters, "No, I like the freedom of doing this myself." She reflected, "I've seen a huge change in me. Before coming to Kandahar Treasure I had accepted my miserable destiny that I would always be living under the command of others. Now I know who I am as an individual."

Zian Jaan defines financial freedom as "earning my own money and spending it as I wish." However, when the men in her household are out of work, a common occurrence in a country with 40 percent unemployment, she generously contributes to buying food and other household needs. She also makes purchases for her son and pays for his schooling. Beyond these contributions, Zia Jaan saves money, saying, "I love to travel." Her eyes sparkle as she tells of trips to Iran, Pakistan, and India. India stood out as a "free country. I could do anything I wanted. Nobody said anything."

Today Zia Jaan is treated like a member of Rangina's extended family, staying overnight when working late, and participating in family events. Zia Jaan especially enjoys joining Rangina and her young daughter in dressing up and attending the women-only dinners that are a central part of the many weddings to which Rangina is invited. Zia Jaan looks forward to the eating, visiting, and dancing among the glittery-dressed women that last well into the wee hours of the morning.

In reminiscing over the changes in her life since coming to Kandahar Treasure, Zia Jaan expanded on her independence and freedom, "I make the choice to come out of the house, to work or not. I don't let anyone tell me anymore what to do, what not to do, or how to do it." Yet, Zia Jaan does not dismiss her family's support as she enters Kandahar's potentially dangerous streets, "Every day that I come out of my house and every day that I go back, I am always looking around my shoulder to see who is after me, who is doing what. But every night I tell my boys. We discuss the security situation and they encourage me to continue going. So that encouragement—it's very important."

Zia Jaan offered tough words to husbands whose households are in dire financial straits but who will not allow their women to come out for work, "If you care so much to keep your women in the home, then provide for them. And if you can't provide, then let your women be able to go out and find a means of income to feed the family and themselves." Zia Jaan expressed gratitude that she can come each day to Kandahar Treasure. With her earnings, she cares for her son and contributes to her household when funds are short. Should she ever experience problems with her stepchildren so that they don't want her in the house, Zia Jaan concluded, "I have a home here at Kandahar Treasure to go to always. I can take care of myself."

FIVE

KANDAHAR TREASURE —
"This is serious work."

*When used by artists in acts of self-determination,
folk art is a powerful instrument of change.
And traditional artists are proving to be formidable change
agents. Yet even tradition needs traction to keep pace in the modern age, and
artists are forced to find innovative solutions that preserve cultural
heritage and keep their communities intact.*

Carmella Padilla, *The Work of Art*

Rangina and her father answered an inner call to assist in the rebuilding of Afghanistan. After nearly twenty-five years of warfare, hopefulness permeated the diaspora, with Hamid Karzai installed as Interim Head of State in 2002. Rangina said, "People were excited and wanted to go back. I wanted to go back too, but I didn't know in what capacity." Returning to Kandahar in July, 2002, Rangina and her father found a city of bombed-out buildings. Bullet holes pierced compound walls. Pavement lay in rubble along former tree-lined streets.

Rangina gave herself three weeks to assess the situation and gauge where she could contribute to the rebuilding efforts. When no opportunities materialized, she returned to the United States, dejected. Knowing his daughter's deep desire for giving back to Afghanistan, Mr. Hamidi contacted his old friend Qayum Karzai, the President's brother. Qayum lived in Columbia, Maryland, and had founded Afghans for Civil Society (ACS), a Maryland-based non-governmental organization (NGO). Learning of Rangina's interest, Qayum offered Rangina a position as Program Manager for the ACS Women's Income Generation Project in Kandahar. Rangina replied, "I'm going. I had this strong desire to work for women. I was so desperate to return that I didn't even ask how much they would pay. All I knew was that there was a house to live in and a place to work." Rangina arrived for the rebuilding in February, 2003; Mr. Hamidi would join the rebuilding efforts four years later as Mayor of Kandahar.

Kandahar Treasure is a creative enterprise, but as a for-profit business, tracking the details is critical. Rangina keeps careful records of goods received, money paid out to the embroiderers, and sales.

Few women in Kandahar Province today are formally educated, but a thumb print is as good as a signature.

ACS charged Rangina with expanding the nonprofit project—at that time a small group of women embroidering to earn money. She launched the expansive goal of women reaching economic self-sufficiency from their embroidery earnings. Over the next five years, Rangina acquired confidence as a young woman working in the development sector, having arrived in Afghanistan "not really knowing what development was." By visiting women's homes to collect khamak, she connected with women's lives and learned of issues and problems they faced.

Initially, Rangina assessed that the quality of the khamak was very poor. She had grown up surrounded by her mother's high quality khamak—scarves, shawls, pants—which her mother wore and admired. Rangina wondered if the poor quality resulted from wartime, when women put little effort into embroidery. But she spotted high quality khamak hidden here and there in Kandahar market stalls and in the homes of women she visited. Over time, she realized that "the ACS women were getting paid, no matter what the quality. And not just with our project, but with so many other projects—those sponsored by the United Nations, and the United States Agency for International Development, among others. The women approached the work with the attitude that said, "Why expend the energy if I'm going to get paid the same amount anyway?" Rangina was young and inexperienced, so she didn't know enough to argue or negotiate with them and say to the women that this was not acceptable.

About a year into the program Rangina insisted, "You do good work or you don't get paid the full price." The women voiced their displeasure and argued that the former program director, an American woman, didn't think the quality was poor. They argued that if an American believed the quality was acceptable, who was Rangina, an Afghan, to reject the work? However, Rangina stood by her demand, as she believed the women could meet her expectations. When she started reducing payments to the women, quality improved.

The ACS nonprofit project garnered funding from various sources. As the project grew, writing grant proposals consumed increasing amounts of Rangina's time. All too often the funders, such as the National Endowment for Democracy, wanted her to include photos of the women in their project reports; yet the women didn't want to be photographed, for cultural reasons. Rangina found writing proposals increasingly problematic, as she was having to deal with funding agency politics that detracted her from working directly with the women in the project.

Over time, product quality continued to improve, and better base fabrics for the embroidery were sought out in Pakistan. Rangina initiated khamak innovations, particularly with motifs and products for marketability in the United States. The project expanded to more than 400 women working in their homes. Then in 2007, an event gave Rangina pause to reconsider her future as a development leader. Back in the United States, her sister and brother-in-law nominated her for a CNN Hero award, one that honors individuals who make extraordinary contributions to humanitarian aid and make a difference in their communities. CNN journalists interviewed Rangina for eight hours as a CNN finalist. From these hours of discussion, CNN writers pulled the phrase "women are treated like animals here" for use in their publicity. From these few words, pulled out of context from a lengthy interview, Rangina was heavily criticized within Afghanistan. Family members who nominated her felt deeply hurt. Following the CNN controversy, Rangina sensed a growing distrust from her superiors. Time devoted to paperwork and grant writing continued to escalate. Finally, tired and dejected, she departed from ACS in 2007.

TRAINING AS A BUSINESS ENTREPRENEUR

During the time Rangina led the Women's Income Generation Project for ACS, she mulled over alternative models for sustainable income generation. Nonprofit, donor agency, or government aid models seemed inadequate for what she hoped to accomplish. In reflecting on her ACS nonprofit experience, she said, "The bureaucracies, the politics, the lack of a real vision forward disappointed me.

In the past thirty years of war and destruction, my country had become a nation of beggars. We constantly were waiting to be spoon-fed by the world. I thought that the alternative was a business model. Business offered sustainability; business allowed people to stand on their own two feet; and business gave people hope to rebuild their lives with their own hands."

Opportunities to participate in two entrepreneurship training programs in 2006 nourished Rangina's refocus toward a business model for development. Project Artemis at Thunderbird School of Global Management, located at Arizona State University, prepared Afghan women in entrepreneurship and business skills. Rangina described her three-week campus residency as a fast paced "mini-MBA where we were introduced to basic business principles. I saw potential to transfer what we were doing as a nonprofit project into a potentially viable business." Topics such as finance, management, branding, advertising, and marketing seemed a good fit for Rangina's evolving business ideas.

A second program, BPeace (Business Council for Peace), applied a fashion perspective to Rangina's emerging business model. Following intensive fashion training at the Fashion Institute of Technology in New York, U.S. business volunteers traveled to Afghanistan for continued entrepreneurship mentoring.

Rangina recalled a pivotal exercise in the BPeace, "Silk Road Fashion Training." Participants were asked to create a meaningful name for their businesses. As Rangina struggled, Toni Maloni, head of BPeace, challenged her to think of something valuable to highlight the intricate khamak handwork. Toni hinted at how customers shopping at Tiffany's in New York associated beautiful, high-quality jewelry with the company name. Rangina identified the word "treasure" to describe the valued khamak embroidery. She also wanted Kandahar as an Afghan identifier. Together they arrived at Kandahar Treasure. When translated to Pashto, it became Kandahari Khazana. Rangina said, "This name would show to Afghan society that this embroidery was something valuable, as the name

khazana was associated with a form of beloved historical poetry that is treasured by Afghans." Beyond the curricular learning that Rangina gained from the two programs, she and other budding Afghan women entrepreneurs were mentored for more than ten years. Rangina still feels she can call on her mentors for ongoing support.

LAUNCHING KANDAHAR TREASURE

Although Rangina had left ACS in 2007, after several months she reconnected with the women with whom she had been working. Rangina stood ready to give birth to Kandahar Treasure as a business enterprise. Kandahar Treasure registered as a for-profit business in January, 2008. The organization's business model, with the dual goals of benefitting the business as well as the broader society, shared similarities with the concept of a B Corp (Benefit Corporation) in the United States.

Kandahar Treasure fits the global definition of a social enterprise—an initiative targeting the neglect of a group of people who lack the means or clout to achieve transformation on their own. Kandahar Treasure worked to revive khamak embroidery as an avenue for generating income for the women who practiced the craft. As such, it exemplified a social enterprise aimed at decreasing marginalization of women in Afghanistan.

Headquartered in a large, two-story building set in an airy compound, the Kandahar workshop includes a manager's office that is used for receiving and inspecting completed work from among the current 300 women who embroider at home; a tailoring room with eight industrial sewing machines, cutting table, and ironing station; a work room where embroiderers sit together on the floor for designing prototypes and where the entire group eats lunch. In addition, there is a prayer room; a kitchen; a storeroom for fabrics, yarns, and other supplies; and an office for the bookkeeper, a man who must work in a separate space from the women.

Rayon floss in vibrant hues takes the place of traditional silk in khamak embroidery.

One of the embroiderers at Kandahar Treasure receives additional income by coming early each day to make bread for the staff.

The twenty-five women employed at the office, ranging in age from fifteen to a little over sixty, arrive each morning at 8:00 am and leave at 4:00 pm. Beginning in 2015, Kandahar Treasure provided transportation through two contract drivers who pick up the women in neighborhoods across the city. In the past, some of the women walked several hours to the office, or, if they had money for transportation, to a public taxi stand. When walking, burqa-clad women often faced contentious sexual harassment. Men whistled, yelled offensive words, or touched the women's bodies. Should a woman respond to the aggravation, others on the street would assume she must have done something to attract the attention. One woman thanked Rangina: "You don't know how much at ease I am going to bed because I don't have to hear all of that every day. I can sleep at night." In addition to feeling safe when traveling to work, the women arrive fresher and complete their work more efficiently.

Kandahar Treasure places a high priority on maintaining a safe and secure workplace for women. The organization maintains zero tolerance for improper behavior by men toward Kandahar Treasure members. Upon the women's arrival at the compound's front gates, male security guards identify the burqa-clad Kandahar Treasure members for entry. Women continue to wear their burqas as they pass through the gate, cross the courtyard, and enter the workshop door. Only then, do the women remove their burqas. Guards remain in their guardhouse near the compound gate, where they monitor visitors or run errands in the city. As the guards cannot see women visitors through their burqas, they use an electronic call system to the office to determine if a visitor should be allowed entrance.

Over time the guards and drivers have become very protective of Kandahar Treasure's women. Rangina shared an example of a guard extending protection to her when an unknown male visitor arrived. To quell his uncertainty about the male visitor, the guard asked if he could sit quietly to the side during the meeting between Rangina and the visitor.

COUNTERING SUSPICIONS

Some members of the public voiced suspicion, despite these protective precautions, as to what kind of work occurred at Kandahar Treasure. People equated Kandahar Treasure with their images of NGOs—corrupt organizations operating in the development sector. They distrusted foreigners who advocated for female independence. Particularly in Kandahar, Afghan women working with

The women of Kandahar Treasure work together to prepare a special dish for an annual charity on Prophet Muhammad's birth.

outsiders in democracy-promoting NGOs were linked with women wearing short skirts, throwing off their head-scarves, smoking, drinking, and sleeping with men.

Because words can easily defeat an organization, Rangina takes great care in how she talks about Kandahar Treasure in public, particularly among men. "When I started working in Kandahar right after the Taliban were driven out in 2003, getting women to consider working outside the home was taboo, and it still is. But when you link the work back to embroidery, then men say, 'Oh, it is just embroidery.' It's not a threat to the social order. So the question doesn't even come into their minds of what women are doing here." However, if Rangina used power-ful words that the international community used—words such as empowering women, teaching women to be inde-pendent—that would alarm the men and they would not

allow their wives to work at Kandahar Treasure.

Expanding on the concept of trust, Rangina noted that the years of warfare have created a society where trust is absent. Once gained, trust can be broken by simple daily acts such as forgetting to don a headscarf, not praying at a requisite hour, or saying the wrong thing at the wrong time. As she said, "This society is not very forgiving, espe-cially of women. So to gain the public's trust, people like me in my position have had to be very careful in the steps we take. It's very easy to make mistakes and be publicly criticized in the first few years when you are starting out. Just as one small mistake in stitching ruins the khamak textile, one small misstep in life puts an end to the trust."

Kandahar Treasure maintains an open-door policy for all family members to visit and tour the women's work-shop. Some husbands remained skeptical that Kandahar

Treasure truly offers a culturally-acceptable place for women to work. Rangina told of a husband who questioned what his wife, an exceptional embroiderer, was doing when she arrived home later than he anticipated. This woman had failed to tell her husband of the seasonal schedule change in working hours. He stormed into Rangina's office. "What kind of office is this? Every office that I know of works until 12:00 noon and you work until 4:00 pm." Rangina waited patiently until he simmered down and then offered him a chair. When she asked the husband if he was a proud Afghan man, he confirmed his cultural identity. She then reminded him that under the Pashtun code of honor, men are to provide financially for their wives and children. Yet here was a woman, heavily pregnant with her ninth daughter, who was walking to work in the summer heat. Apparently the family, composed of the man's three wives and many children, desperately needed the worker's earnings. After hearing about the seasonal working hours and viewing the secluded workspace, the man quieted down, saying "I am so sorry. I thought this was a different place. I have never heard of this kind of place." The woman returned the next day, smiling, and shared that her husband now was offering praise for the kind of place where his wife worked.

Kandahar Treasure's positive story slowly spread as families gained confidence about their women's workplace treatment and benefited from the consistent income women brought to their households. They also visually substantiated the nature of the work through the beautiful embroidered products they saw displayed in retail stores. Rangina said, "Now the families and people know that we are not acting like their image of an NGO. We are providing work to poor women. We are paying them on time and fairly. We are treating them all equally. We are doing what we have said we were doing for the past ten years." Zia Jaan, a long-time Kandahar Treasure member, said, "I am happy to be in an office that keeps my honor in mind and it's a very honorable place to work. My family is proud of me. And, I'm proud of myself to be working in such an organization."

DAILY ROUTINES

Over the course of each busy day, up to thirty women who work at home return their completed embroidery. A traffic jam materializes in the manager's office as the work is inspected, payment made, and new work distributed. Fareba, the manager, and her assistants inspect each piece for cleanliness and exactness of design execution. Because of the persistent dust in household compounds, many pieces acquire slight blemishes. Pieces are rejected only if there is a severe stain. Fareba also holds the textiles up to the light to check for any random holes that the women may have poked into the fabric with a needle. Provided that the piece meets Kandahar Treasure's standards of quality, the woman is paid immediately. The final finishing of washing and ironing by workshop staff readies the products for sale.

Each woman's earnings are entered on her individual record and documented by her signature or thumbprint. A copy of each transaction is given to the women. As most of the women are illiterate, what they do with the receipt is unknown. Recently one woman told Rangina she threw the receipts away immediately when she left the office. As she said, "What am I going to do with them?" Rangina asked her if she knew how much she earned over six months, and suggested that she have someone in her household help her with the addition. The woman countered, "If I see that [the total] and I find that I made a lot of money and I've spent it all or wasted it, then I will feel bad." Rangina suggested an alternative scenario. If she knew how much she made and got into a fight with her husband where he called her a worthless being, she could show her total earnings with the retort, "Stop blaming me because here is my contribution to the family." The woman thought for a few minutes, smiled, and affirmed she was going to keep her paper receipts from that day forward.

Provided that the completed embroidery a woman brings to the office passes inspection, she is given new work. The designs for all Kandahar Treasure products are photocopied and collected in thick notebooks that are stored in the Kandahar Treasure office. The designs

Rangina takes great care in how she talks about Kandahar Treasure in public, particularly among men.

are then distributed to women as they come to the office to return finished embroidery and pick up new work for completion at home.

For the twenty-five salaried women in the office, their busy workdays are interspersed with opportunities for tea and for midday prayers in the room set aside for private observance. All women join together for a daily lunch of bread; a main dish of eggplant, spinach, okra, or other seasonal vegetable; and a yogurt drink. Offering a lunch ensures that no women go hungry during the day. Were the lunch not provided, some of the poorest women would likely not bring a lunch, choosing instead to put their earnings toward feeding their children. Whenever possible, Kandahar Treasure offers additional income-generating opportunities to women who work within the organization. One woman, a particularly good bread maker, is paid to make fresh bread each morning on an outdoor tabakhai. When another woman saved enough money to buy a cow for her family, Kandahar Treasure hired her to process some of the milk for the women's daily lunchtime yogurt.

In order to ensure time for organizational planning, Thursdays are set aside as days when no outside women are allowed to bring their completed work to the office for inspection and payment. Rather, the salaried women in the office use the day to review the past week's activities, assess raw material supplies, prepare embroidery packets for distribution to women working at home, and plan for the next week's production. Packets include all the necessary materials to complete a piece, such as a measured and hemmed scarf, colored threads for embroidery, and a colored photocopy of the design. Some of the embroidery experts can work directly from a photocopy while others, who are less skilled, need an embroidered prototype for guidance. The office closes on Friday, a Muslim holy day.

One of two Kandahar Treasure retail stores in Kandahar, this one is located in a well-to-do neighborhood where women can afford to buy their khamak rather than stitch it themselves.

BEYOND DAILY ROUTINES

Collective discussion among the manager, Fareba, and several master embroiderers guides pricing of new designs and products. The group examines the new design for its financial potential, based on the difficulty of embroidery execution and the likely time required. New, intricate designs are reserved for the top, most highly skilled master embroiderers. Simpler designs go to women with more limited abilities.

When a woman receives a new order, a tag is attached to the piece, displaying the Kandahar Treasure logo, and giving the organization's telephone number, price to be paid for the completed work, and thread colors. Women with adolescent daughters of marriageable age, who are not allowed to leave their compounds, pick up pieces for their family members. Sometimes there is a question of whether the daughter has received the piece. Instead, the woman may give a 1000-afghani piece to a neighbor to embroider. When she receives payment at the Kandahar Treasure office for the completed work, she will pay 300 afghanis to the neighbor and then pocket the 700-afghani remainder. While Kandahar Treasure cannot prevent women removing the tag, they hope that a detailed tag attached to the textile helps to curtail such practice. As Rangina said, "We are trying our best to be as open and transparent in our financial dealings as possible, but it's not perfect."

New members are added infrequently; only as markets grow are new embroiderers invited. Kandahar Treasure relies on a word-of-mouth referral system, primarily through neighbors of existing members. When a potential new member arrives, she is asked about her family and about whether family members are working. Questions are posed to help ensure that the new member is not employing other women from whom she is profiting. If a woman says she has a daughter who needs work, the organization asks the daughter to come to the office for an embroidery audition. She is given a small embroidery sample to sit in the office and complete as evidence of her skills.

Beyond the financial benefits for the women, Rangina would like to create more ways for the women to support and learn from each other. Security issues in the city prevent the entire group of Kandahar Treasure women from gathering for a meeting in a common location; unwanted attention could arise from outsiders in the community. In a smaller initiative, a shura (council) was created of nine women who worked at home and who were most active in their communities. The women generated ideas they wanted to discuss. For the first half-year, the group met monthly for two to three hours to discuss Kandahar Treasure-related issues. When Rangina suggested they expand their discussion to social issues, the women expressed reluctance. They associated such discussion with political bodies—clearly something they wanted to avoid. The women were aware that when other organizations called women together for meetings or discussion, the organizations provided lunch and covered their transportation costs. Kandahar Treasure was not in a position to offer these financial incentives. When there was no monetary benefit, women eventually lost interest in the shura's continuation.

ESTABLISHING MARKETS

As with other artisan organizations around the world, establishing multiple channels for retail sales locally and abroad contributes to long-term enterprise sustainability. All too often artisan groups become dependent on one retail format, which can lead to dramatic financial instability during political and economic volatility, as has occurred in Afghanistan. The intricate nature of high quality khamak embroidery means that it is high priced. During Afghanistan's wartime period, purchasing khamak became out of reach for most Afghan consumers. Marketing to foreigners working within Afghanistan and to customers outside the country became critical to offset dwindling local sales.

Kandahar Treasure has tried four types of retail channels, some with more success than others. These include gift markets, retail stores, international fairs, and in-home

Festive dresses, embroidered with tribal motifs and mirror work, are part of the product mix at one Kandahar Treasure shop.

sales. Khamak embroidery is heavily used in gift-giving in Afghanistan. In a country and culture known for its hospitality, guests are not only treated with respect but also are offered gifts when leaving the house. Common gifts for respected guests might include an embroidered scarf or pants for women and an embroidered tunic for boys and men. This gift-giving practice sustains the demand and market for embroidered gift items.

Rangina's father, as Mayor of Kandahar, participated in the hospitality of gift-giving for visitors to the city. He supported Kandahar Treasure by purchasing khamak embroidered yokes, scarves, and shawls for the many guests he received in his leadership role. When the Governor of Kandahar District saw the textiles, he, too, started buying to fulfill his gift-giving obligations. On several occasions, especially when President Karzai visited Kandahar, these orders rose to 250 yokes for men's tunics in a single sales transaction. In addition to the gift itself, prestige is enhanced by how the gift is wrapped. Kandahar Treasure women jumped

on the opportunity to provide this value-added service for the officials' khamak embroidered gifts.

A fortuitous gift which Mayor Hamidi presented to the military commander at the NATO airbase in Kandahar led to their first retail store. The commander asked why Kandahar Treasure was not selling at the base. He first offered a tiny container space for retail sales. Kandahar Treasure expanded to a larger shop as their sales to members of the military grew. The military base shop assisted Kandahar Treasure in learning about customer interest among foreigners. Scarves in a variety of sizes sold well for soldiers to take home as gifts to women in their families. Requests from African American soldiers for dolls with darker skin puzzled the Afghan women in a country where light skin is valued, "Why would you make a dark fabric doll? Who would want to buy them for America?" Despite skepticism, the women produced the dolls and they sold well.

As United States troop deployment in Afghanistan began to draw down in 2014, Kandahar Treasure consid-

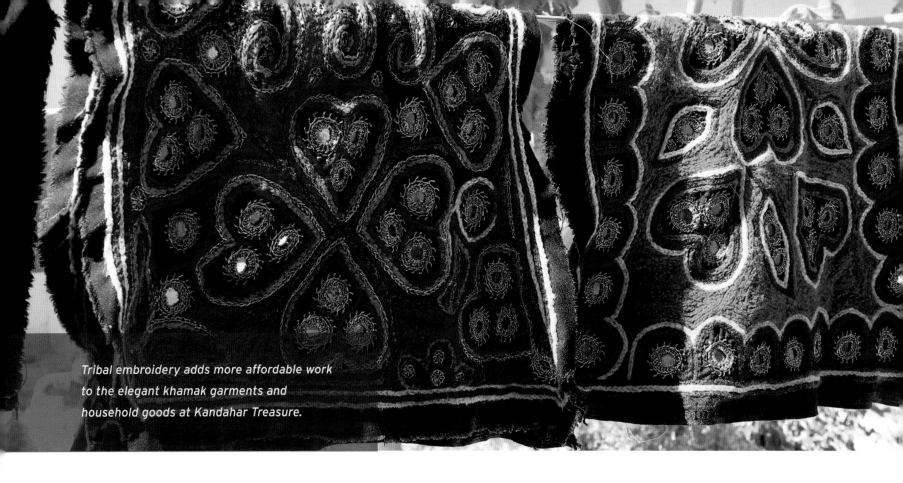

Tribal embroidery adds more affordable work to the elegant khamak garments and household goods at Kandahar Treasure.

ered new retail options. Aino Mina, a sprawling, upscale housing development with a park-like setting opened on the outskirts of Kandahar. For their store in Aino Mina, Kandahar Treasure switched from their focus on foreigners to products for domestic customers. The shop, opened in 2014, specializes in embroidered baby layettes, wedding sets for brides' new homes, and shawls. Men's embroidered yokes are packaged with matching fabric for customers to take to a tailor for sewing. In 2016, Kandahar Treasure opened a second shop in the central women's market—Rang Rezan, the old market for the dyeing and pleating of burqas. They hope to expand sales to a broader market than the high-end customers living in Aino Mina.

To attract women to their new shop in the women's market, Kandahar Treasure needed to create a store environment that was safe and welcoming to women. Services offered in the shop included two welcoming saleswomen from Kandahar Treasure, a carpet for sitting, prayer rugs, water, and a bathroom facility nearby. With a woman shopkeeper, female customers felt comfortable raising the front of their burqas to examine products first-hand. Unfortunately, with Afghanistan's stagnant economy, both stores have struggled to attract customers to the fine-quality khamak textiles.

Kandahar Treasure' first foray into direct international sales began in 2006 and has continued each summer for twelve years. The rigorously juried International Folk Art Market in Santa Fe, New Mexico, accepts approximately 25 percent of the applications from artists working to sustain their folk art traditions around the world. Kandahar Treasure's high quality embroidery and unique products have been reviewed favorably, with invitations to return to the market year after year.

Prior to the Folk Art Market, sales in the United States were mostly charity-based; sellers told the women's story and asked customers to buy in support of the women. In contrast, the International Folk Art Market sales broadened Rangina's understanding of U.S. customer behavior. "That proved to me that our story was important, but the quality was really important too. People care about the craftsmanship. They respond with awe to the fineness of the work. It has given me this boost to say that we are actually doing something important. There is something more to this than it is just work done by Afghan women." Participation in the market has led to further quality enhancements, creation of new products, and design and color changes for U.S. customers. The market has supported Kandahar Treasure's branding of their products as fine-quality, expensive embroidery. In addition to sales, Rangina has benefitted from the many contacts she has made among apparel industry members who attend the market and have become Kandahar Treasure supporters. Since their success in Santa Fe, Kandahar Treasure has also participated in folk art markets in India and on the U.S. military base in Ramstein, Germany.

In-home or conference sales in the United States also have helped to tell the story of Kandahar Treasure and to generate small sales. When she is in the United States, Rangina and her sister, who lives in the Washington, D.C. area, host these sales. Rangina also receives invitations to speak on university campuses or at conferences; she always takes products for sale. She finds that university students, with their expanding focus on socially conscious buying, are intrigued with the Kandahar Treasure story as well as being attracted to the high-quality products.

In gauging impacts from Kandahar Treasure's various retail channels, Rangina notes that the retail shops in Kandahar have helped the women to understand the bigger picture of what they do. She explained, "Even though I tell them about sales abroad, it's hard for the women to understand. But the local shops are something they visit; they see the customers coming in and buying. They talk with customers who come to the workshop for a commissioned special order. It's not a dream, something out of their reach. They see that our shops are clean and offer products of high quality and in color combinations that are appealing—all a strong contrast to the lower-quality products displayed in other less attractive shops in Kandahar."

BECOMING PROFESSIONALS

After nearly ten years with Kandahar Treasure, Rangina understands that creating an operational team of women with different but complementary skills for designing, embroidering, and tailoring has been critical to their success. The fulltime staff members are aware that they are becoming more organized and professional. Now, each new product design is executed in a series of color options and sizes to meet market demand in Afghanistan and abroad. In Afghanistan, with embroidery considered to be women's work, khamak had never before been considered a professional pursuit. The women perceive that they are not just coming and wasting a day and getting a salary because they are women and working. Now, the women take responsibility to fulfill their tasks as part of a larger organization that requires each person's contribution to be successful. Rangina said, "That level of understanding with the women is huge. If you don't have that, you cannot call any project 'development'."

For most of the women at Kandahar Treasure, their previous interactions with other women were entirely within their households. Bickering among sisters, mothers, daughters, daughters-in-law, and co-wives commonly erupted. Rangina has intervened to let the women know, "This is not a home. You are not sisters-in-law at home fighting over stupid little things. This is a workplace where you need to learn to put aside your differences to get things accomplished."

Rangina summarizes, "Working within the cultural system is crucial to being successful in Kandahar, no matter what you are doing." The organization is quietly creating a supportive network of women working together in a safe environment and toward a common goal. The women are seeing that their work is valuable, not just financially to themselves, but to their customers. They are reviving an important Afghan textile tradition. As one of the full-time women remarked, "This is serious work."

A MOTHER AND DAUGHTER FIND FREEDOM

MUZLIFA AND GULSIKA

Muzlifa's mother, Gulsika, didn't want to teach her daughter to embroider khamak. So Muzlifa observed carefully and then snuck behind her mother's back to practice the stitches. As Eid approached, Muzlifa surprised her mother with a little yoke, a gift she embroidered for her younger brother to wear during the celebrations. Gulsika acknowledged her daughter's talent. "From then on, I said, do as you wish. And she has been embroidering khamak ever since." Today, at age fifteen, Muzlifa works mornings at Kandahar Treasure, applying her considerable talents to prototyping new khamak designs. In the afternoons, she attends school as a fourth grader studying nine subjects.

Muzlifa is an accomplished embroiderer and a successful student, thanks to her persistence and her mother's bold decisions. Still, like the women in this photo, neither woman is comfortable showing her face in public.

In joining Kandahar Treasure, mother and daughter faced challenging cultural transitions. Widowed and with three children, Gulsika lived with her mother and married brother in a typical Kandahari household. Men made the decisions and women remained at home. Men did not look favorably on a young girl such as Muzlifa attending school, despite her badly wanting to learn. Her mother's options for income generation remained limited as well because she was restricted to the household. Yet Gulsika, a master tailor, persisted and asked a neighbor to introduce her to Kandahar Treasure. She heard it was a place where only women worked. Gulsika says, "My need taught me how to tailor. Making my children's clothes had been my greatest need, so I learned by myself. I haven't been to class or training."

Slowly, the family accepted Gulsika's working outside the household and welcomed her income. However, problems arose when Gulsika took Muzlifa with her to the workshop. Rangina was offering daughters of Kandahar Treasure staff a chance to apprentice with the organization, and Gulsika felt this offered her daughter a valuable opportunity. Gulsika initially told her brother and mother what she was doing, and they did not offer objections. However, after only four days, their feelings changed, and Gulsika's mother threw the family of four out of the house. The mother expressed fear that with two women leaving the house each morning and returning in the afternoon, extremists might shoot the man of the house, her son, for allowing such behaviors. The mother's ultimatum, "Stay here and do not work, or get out."

Reflecting on the demand, Gulsika recalled that each day when she returned home, she found Muzlifa exhausted and begging to lie down. Only then did she realize that her ten-year-old daughter was carrying water from a neighborhood well several times a day, cooking, cleaning, washing, and taking care of the other children. The mother and sister-in-law were losing their household drudge with Muzlifa's working at Kandahar Treasure. To further compound the hostility, Gulsika courageously demanded that if she was forced to leave, she should receive her share of the house her father had built. Mullahs and community elders gathered to discuss the appropriate compensation.

Gulsika describes the share they granted her as equal to the "width of a door." Angered by the decision, Gulsika packed her suitcases and fled with her children.

Gulsika found a one-bedroom rental house and hasn't looked back, "We are happy. I don't have to listen to anyone's complaints or bickering. I never dreamed I would be on my own with all my children, ages twelve, thirteen, and fifteen, attending school."

At work, Muzlifa values the opportunity to develop prototypes with her exquisite stitching and creative designs, "It's much more enjoyable than repeating the same design over." Carefully observing her mother when she was a young girl has paid off, despite her mother's early reluctance to teach her. "I used to pay very close attention to what she was doing and how she was doing it. It just stayed with me and that's how I learned." Mother's and daughter's income from Kandahar Treasure now supports their household of four living independently.

As Gulsika, Muzlifa, Rangina, and I sat talking, Rangina shared that she and other women with similar educational backgrounds encourage and mentor young girls

to attend school. However, culturally it is really not their place, as outsiders to the girls' families, to do so. In counseling the girls, Rangina warns, "In the process of getting yourself educated, don't do other smaller things that will attract negative attention. Be careful in the other choices you make. You've already made a big one." Rangina discourages dressing in a way to look different than people around them, behaving in ways that do not fit in with the masses, or trying to choose their own husbands and running away. She says, "The girls have broken one boundary in going to school, but we are promoting that they stay within other cultural norms."

Turning back to our discussion of Muzlifa's schooling, she reported that she did very well in her first year of school—the third grade. When I congratulated her, Muzlifa shyly thanked me for being happy about her studies—perhaps a response that she rarely receives outside Kandahar Treasure and her immediate family. Looking to the future, Muzlifa wants to be a teacher. "What I know, I want to teach others."

Gulsika smiled, "I'll be happy with whatever she is happy doing."

KHAMAK *as a* LIVING TRADITION

In the artist's resilient and resourceful hands,
traditional art becomes a cultural lifeline.

Carmella Padilla, *The Work of Art*

Only one basic stitch—satin stitch—is required for khamak embroidery. Yet this simplicity belies a textile tradition that combines stitched motif boundaries and filling designs of immense complexity. Khamak involves counting and covering a set number of threads in the background fabric with embroidered stitches in a prescribed order. One miscount ruins the entire design. The mistake can be corrected only by removing the stitches back to their origin. Rangina explained, "In a woman's life, one small mistake, such as coming out of the house by herself or without a burqa, costs her. It can ruin her reputation for the rest of her life. No matter how much the woman repents, no matter how much of a good person she becomes, once she is tainted she is tainted for life. With khamak work, you can take it out and go back. Unfortunately, in life, you cannot rewind and go back."

Our goal in this chapter is to place the needlework practice of khamak embroidery in a cultural context. To accomplish this, we delved into lively discussions with

Kandahar Treasure women ranging in age from fifteen to their sixties. Women described how they learned khamak as young girls, found sources for design innovation, defined quality, benefited from their earnings, and felt about elevating khamak embroidery to museum-quality status. Although this chapter also offers an overview of the basic technique of khamak, it does not provide "how to" instruction that would be expected in a detailed, process-oriented publication. Rather, the women explain how doing khamak embroidery—as work of honor and work of love—has become a "cultural lifeline" of meaning with significant impact in their lives.

LEARNING KHAMAK—"I loved my needle."

Girls begin learning embroidery at the early age of six or seven. They learn from their mothers or from a sister, aunt, or older relative residing in the compound. Other girls sneak away to learn on their own, stealing a needle,

This vivid embroidery shows the perils of inaccurate counting. Lovely at first glance, a careful look shows where the pattern counting has strayed. This drastically affects the value of the piece. Can you see the flaw?

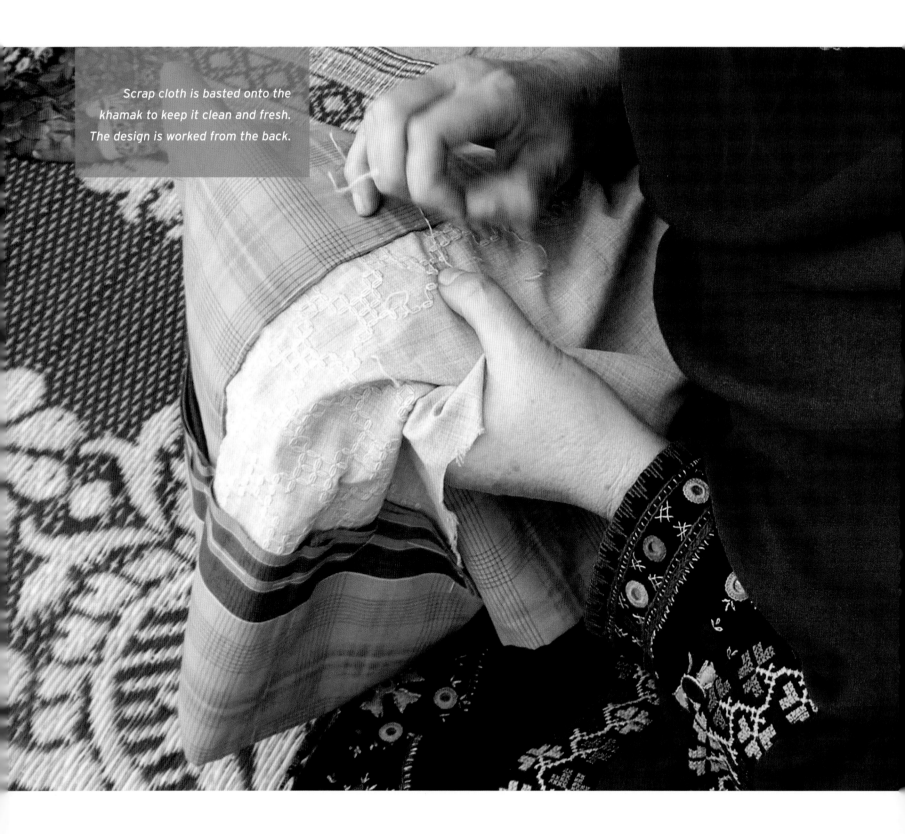

Scrap cloth is basted onto the
khamak to keep it clean and fresh.
The design is worked from the back.

thread, and scrap of fabric from a mother or sister to get started. Or sometimes mothers send daughters to a neighbor who is a master embroiderer. In the master's house, girls sit quietly and focus their attention on learning the complex process of khamak embroidery.

Typically, girls begin their embroidery with a sampler of stitches and patterns. Using fat, colored yarns, they practice satin stitches on a large scale that will eventually diminish in size as the girls become more proficient. Folklore about learning khamak prescribes that once a girl completes a sampler, she should then float it down a stream of water. The clearness of water is said to contribute to continued clarity in the girl's khamak stitches. Other interpretations suggested "your stitches will be like running water—smooth, and flowing constantly" or "by throwing the work in running water you will continue to improve."

As we asked the women to share personal anecdotes about learning to embroider, smiles came to their faces. Jamila remembered that she was sent to a neighbor's house to learn. On the second day, when she wasn't doing well and messed up a design, the neighbor poked her with a needle—a prickly warning that other women recalled receiving as well. Jamila never returned to the neighbor, but stayed at home and practiced, using her mother's khamak as a model.

Several women revealed that they loved doing khamak from the time they first held a needle. One girl would grab work from older women in the household and try to do the work for them. Finally her mother saw her interest, gave her a fabric scrap, and offered a needle to do her own work, so that she would no longer spoil the work of accomplished embroiderers. She said, "My mother got me the fabric and I was the happiest child on the earth. I didn't go outside to play. I was working on that piece of fabric morning and night. I loved my needle. My brother would bring me different colors of thread. Putting the colors together on the fabric was even more fun."

Fareba's mother, concerned with the fighting going on in the streets during wartime, looked for ways to keep her daughters inside. Fareba, who had never held a needle,

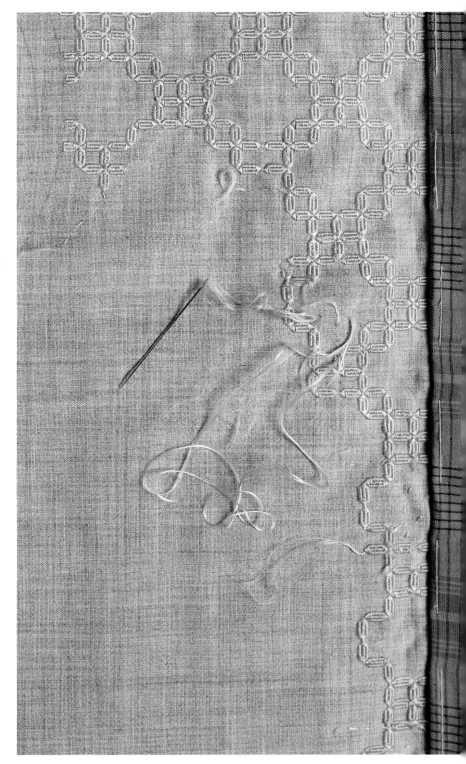

Several women revealed that they loved doing khamak from the time they first held a needle.

became excited when presented with a rainbow of colored threads to embroider what she thought would be fabric for her doll house. However, as it was Fareba's first piece, her mother insisted that she float it in the water. As there was no stream nearby, she took it outside to the muddy ditch in front of her house. She stuck it in the water, but when it didn't float away in several days, she brought it back inside.

Now a master embroiderer, Fareba reflected that from the beginning her embroidery was about showing her talent, "When I was a child, I was always competing to create a new design to have something that my friends didn't have. I wanted to show myself through new work." However, as a child she sometimes became discouraged, "I didn't see any benefit from my work. If I made a yoke, I didn't wear it. It was for men. If I made the white pants, I didn't wear them as a kid. They were for older women. But now, over the years I have seen the benefit, especially here at Kandahar Treasure."

Young girls would often take their embroidery outside and practice while sitting with their friends near the doorways of their compounds. Malalai embroidered even farther afield. Her father, a farmer, worked his land in the mornings and evenings. In the afternoons, when he wanted to rest, he sent Malalai to sit in the field and watch that others did not steal his crops. Before leaving home, she would sneak out a small pink napkin, as she didn't want her mother or sisters to know she was learning khamak. While sitting in the field, she would practice her new art,

covering the entire napkin with stitches. One day her uncle walked by and turned on the water pump near where she was sitting. The water force drove away her fabric, needle, and thread. No longer could she surprise her mother and sisters with what she had learned. Although she didn't purposely float her fabric in a stream, she lost her embroidery to water.

While some mothers reluctantly taught their daughters to embroider, Saibo Khala's family members actively blocked her from learning embroidery. The child of a father with multiple wives, she was barred from joining her own mother and brother when they moved to the city. The stepmothers wanted her to remain in the village to do their housework. Although Saibo Khala's stepsisters were learning khamak and embellishing their pants with beautiful embroidery, they refused to teach her. They didn't want her to embroider nice clothing for herself. The stepsisters' reluctance fomented Saibo Khala's desire to learn khamak even more. To achieve her goal, she would leave the house, telling the family that she was taking the little children out to the street to play. Instead, she would go to her relative's home, leaving the children to their own devices, and learn from the other women who were willing to teach her.

In addition to teaching daughters a skill that is essential for creating a bridal trousseau, some mothers view learning khamak as a way to protect their adolescent daughters' reputations. One woman explained, "Our culture doesn't like girls to be out on the street. Khamak is a process to keep girls from all the messes they could get into. Any mother who wants to protect her daughter's reputation and keep her from doing dangerous things outside makes her do khamak. It keeps her busy."

Regardless of how women began their embroidery, they agreed that learning khamak takes a lifetime. The basic satin stitch is easy to learn. However, how the stitches are counted and combined into border and filling patterns calls for precise and persistent practice of the art. Yet time for focused concentration can be hard to set aside amidst caring for large families and completing household chores.

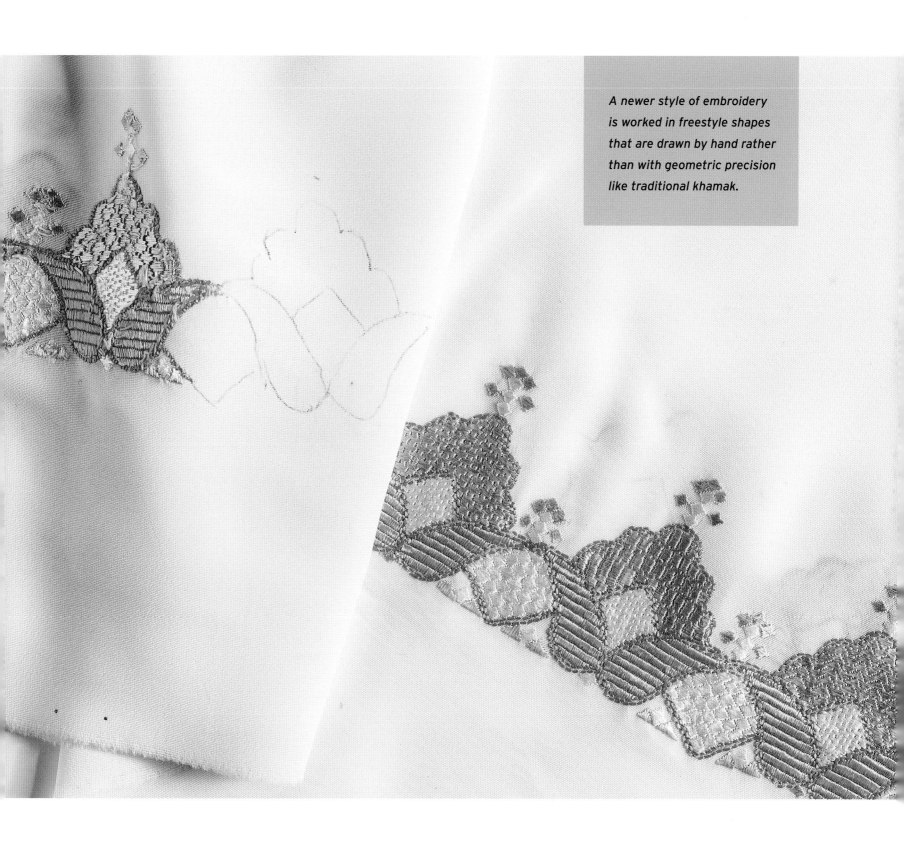

A newer style of embroidery is worked in freestyle shapes that are drawn by hand rather than with geometric precision like traditional khamak.

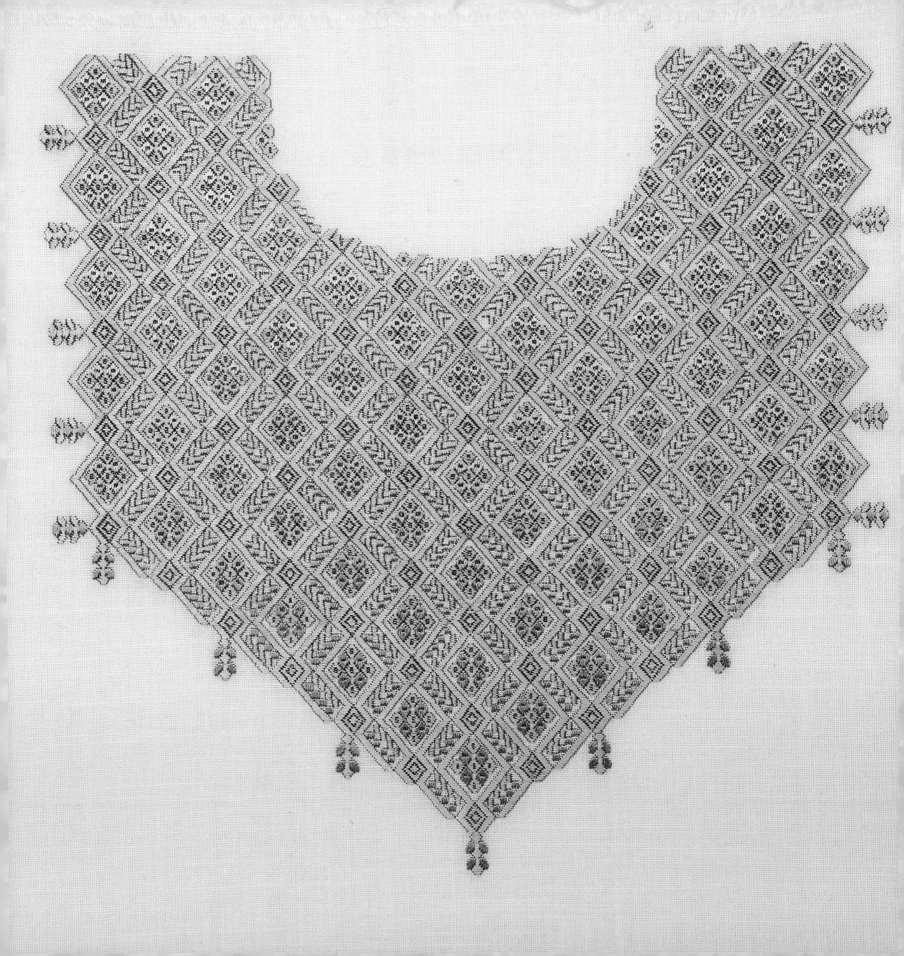

A KHAMAK PRIMER

While it's not our intention to give instructions for how to do khamak, it's important to understand a little bit of how it's done—the challenges it presents, the skills it requires, the inherent value it contains. So imagine this:

You have a piece of fine fabric, rayon and cotton blend, or in former times, perhaps silk. Your fabric has a thread count of 144 to 160 or more: that is, 72 to 80 warp threads and an equal number of weft threads per inch. Your embroidery thread is a fine, slick rayon or silk untwisted floss. Your task is to create a small yoke for a baby brother.

First, you sketch the shape of the yoke. Then you determine a lower midpoint from which all of your entire pattern will extend. Having an idea of your design in mind, you begin to count. Yes, count! Thread by thread, you count from your midpoint to the first boundary point. From that point, you work diagonally to create the first leg of a diamond; and so your work proceeds, dividing your fabric into perfect shapes, the boundaries within which you will create designs.

You are working from the backside of your fabric. There's no frame or hoop to hold it taut. Sitting on the floor, you use your knee to keep the fabric smooth and without slack. It's up to you to make sure there's no pulling or puckering. As you pierce the fabric with your needle and swiftly pull the floss through, you hear a faint "whoosh" that tells you the floss is perfectly even and perfectly tensioned as it settles into its place on the front of the work. That perfection will show in the sheen of the design you are creating. Poorly tensioned stitches will look dull by comparison.

And so your work proceeds. "Whoosh. Whoosh." The needle passes through the carefully-counted intersections where warp and weft cross, and even one miscount can

Every stitch is a testament to the skill
and loving care you are investing
in this gift, a gift that will say,
"This is a child of Kandahar."

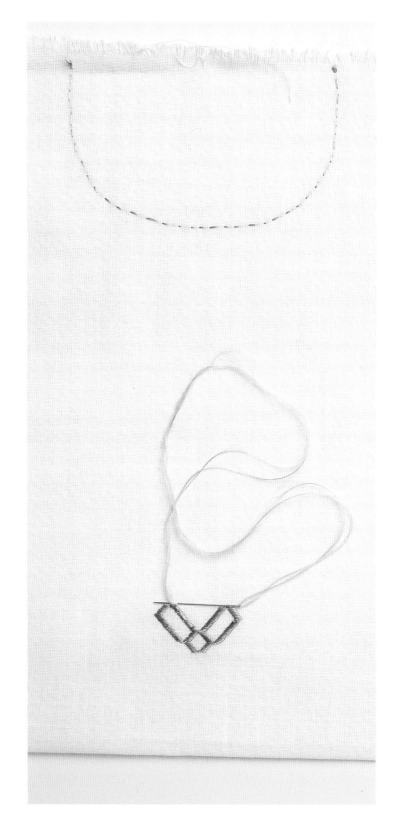

mean taking the work out, stitch by stitch, backing up to where you made the error.

Once the framework is complete, you work a small motif in the center of each diamond—counting carefully to make sure it is perfectly centered. Then you work motifs into the next largest areas. Finally, you fill the remaining space with a solid filling pattern—the choices are endless.

Thousands of carefully-counted stitches later, you finish the edges of the yoke with delicate floral motifs. Then it's ready to be fashioned into a little tunic.

Never mind that you're working without artificial light, never mind that you've not been to school to formally learn your numbers. You count perfectly, you execute perfectly. Every stitch is a testament to the skill and loving care you are investing in this gift, a gift that will say, "This is a child of Kandahar."

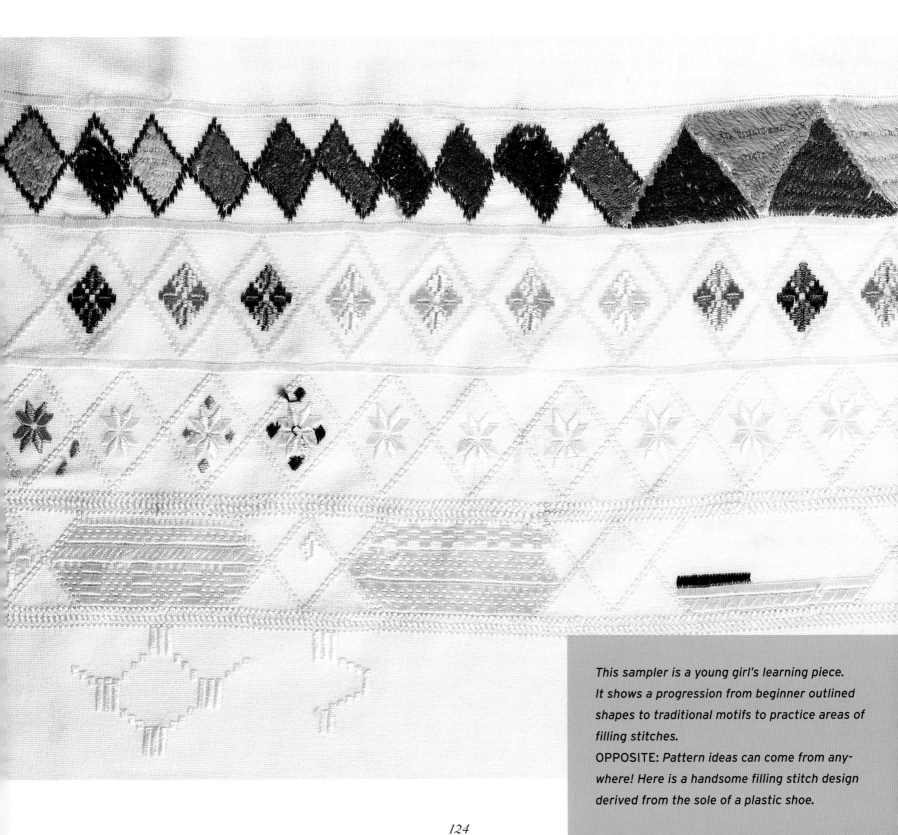

This sampler is a young girl's learning piece. It shows a progression from beginner outlined shapes to traditional motifs to practice areas of filling stitches.

OPPOSITE: Pattern ideas can come from anywhere! Here is a handsome filling stitch design derived from the sole of a plastic shoe.

DESIGNS

Traditional khamak embroidery is limited to geometric motifs only. The base fabric is woven of vertical warp and horizontal weft threads, so the counted satin stitches of the traditional designs must follow this grid. However, in the 1980s, after the Russian invasion, millions of Afghans left Afghanistan to seek refuge in the neighboring country of Pakistan, and khamak embroidery saw innovation for the first time. Exposure to new techniques and designs in Pakistan encouraged khamak embroiderers to try new ideas themselves. Artisans maintained the basic khamak process of counting satin stiches, but the boundaries of the designs were drawn in with a pen and resembled curvilinear shapes of nature—flowers, leaves, trees—popular themes used in Pakistani embroideries. Another popular shape drawn and filled with fine embroidery was a heart. This new style of design quickly gained popularity among the Afghan diaspora in Pakistan. Eventually the designs found their way back to Kandahar where they were popular for almost two decades—lasting until the early 2000s.

When Rangina returned to Kandahar in 2003 and started to analyze the embroidery capabilities of the women artisans, she immediately recognized the use of the basic curved designs drawn and filled with fine embroidery. Remembering her mother's fine pieces of traditional khamak with their geometric borders encouraged her to ask the women to revive their traditional skills rather than creating drawn-in embroidery shapes. Some of the women immediately asked, "Why do you want to bring back what our mothers and grandmothers used to do?" Surprised by the women's question and determined to give the women artisans a journey back to their traditions, Rangina simply replied, "Because those designs were more beautiful than these." The women revived the long-practiced geometric designs, and by 2004 the entire population of Kandahar was returning to traditional designs and motifs and eschewing the drawn-in designs. As members of the Afghan diaspora started to return back to their homeland they

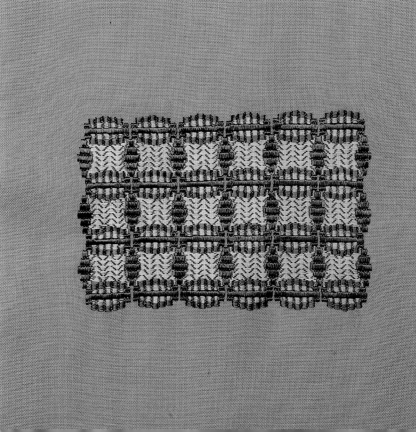

126

Paindo, a Kandahar Treasure embroiderer with fine creative skills, works on an original design. The final piece was sold at the International Folk Art Market in Santa Fe, for a handsome sum.

wore and admired the traditional designs that had defined them as Afghans. Among these are:

KAZA – *"zigzag" as the pattern looks*

COOKNAR – *is the name given to the flower with eight petals and is the popular poppy flower in Kandahar. The shape of the flower is viewed from the top of the poppy flower base.*

GHAMAI – *"diamond" for a diamond shaped pattern*

SHAAKHLA – *"branch" of flower plant*

Kandahar Treasure takes pride in the fact that it is largely responsible for the revival of traditional khamak. They proudly pursue maintaining tradition while encouraging innovation through tradition. Innovation, however, is self-censored by the women embroiderers. Two product requests have been turned down by the artisans—one for an embroidered dog cover and one for an embroidered bikini. Afghan culture views dogs as filthy animals and anything associated with a dog is considered a disgrace. When an order from the West came to embroider dog coats, the women were offended and refused to make a sample. Similarly, they were disgusted when an idea for a khamak embroidered bikini set was presented to them. Kandahari women artisans innovate within boundaries—keeping their cultural sensitivities in mind while foregoing financial opportunities, in order to retain their pride and honor as Afghan citizens.

DESIGN INSPIRATION

While many women become technically proficient embroiderers, only a smaller number exhibit the initiative and creativity for design innovation. As Rangina notes, "Many of the Kandahar Treasure women can precisely copy an existing embroidery design, but only a smaller number can

create or innovate." The women of Kandahar Treasure have grown up in a culture where men tell women what to do in all aspects of their lives. The women have not been encouraged to break out from these demands. For women to flex their imagination represents a small but brave step.

Translation of Kandahar Treasure's new 2016 branding logo from a paper design to an embroidered replica illustrated the women's differing capabilities. The new graphic element incorporated a large triangular assemblage composed of smaller triangles in a rainbow of colors. Rangina challenged several embroiderers to translate the paper illustration to an embroidered version. Woman after woman tried but found it difficult to make the triangles or to match the thread colors exactly to the illustration. However, one of the young, expert embroiderers could make the translation at first try. As Rangina said, "She looked at it and just got it."

Kandahar Treasure embroiderers enjoy doing both older and newer designs. One woman said, "I like to do them both. When I do the older designs, it reminds me of my mom, my grandma. It gives life to my past. When I do new designs, I like that too. It's modernity, new life, new things. For new designs... I take them from my heart."

For those embroiderers who create new designs, inspiration arises from many sources. Looking at old khamak pieces sparks interpretation into a new motif configuration. A flower motif might be cut in half and the halves rearranged for a more contemporary look. Playing with color—going from a monochrome of white on white to adding new colors—creates a different look, and people see it as a new design. Transferring designs from another embroidery technique, such as mirror work, into khamak embroidery appears original and fresh.

Embroiderers also find inspiration in everyday objects around them—prayer rugs and carpets, the textured underside of women's black plastic sandals, a decorative glass pitcher, or designs on printed fabrics sold in the market. One woman recalled a design she created from her chemistry class at school. The molecular structure sparked the idea to create the boundaries for a new embroidery design. Kandahar Treasure applied the designs to scarves for men.

Fareba, the workshop manager, urges embroiderers to consider trial and error with new stitch configurations. If the arrangement appeals to the eye, it remains. If not, the embroiderer is advised to keep working with the design until it is attractive. She warns, however, that creativity requires concentration. Innovation does not emerge when household uproar surrounds the embroiderer—a condition that is common in many Kandahari households.

Regardless of the source for design inspiration, women are careful to protect their new designs from prying neighbors who may want to copy. Rangina explains, "When women create new designs, the innovation is admired by the other women. However, the newness dies very quickly if it is copied almost immediately. It's done. It's gone. It's as if it's not important, which is linked to how the culture views women."

The Kandahar Treasure logo has been adapted for use on gift bags, which emphasizes the value of the work. OPPOSITE: This closeup view shows the fineness of the stitching. The base fabric has about 70 to 72 threads per inch in each direction.

DEFINING QUALITY

High-quality khamak embroidery exhibits a range of characteristics. The design must be counted correctly; no stitches can be off. In a high-quality embroidered piece, the back of the work looks as good as the front. The embroidery threads must shine on the surface. The word khamak means raw, untwisted, or unspun. Twisted threads would be easier to use for embroidery, as they would not catch when pulled through the fabric. However, twisted threads do not produce the flat, shining surface so desired by khamak customers. An accomplished embroider adds that while some khamak exhibits all three of these characteristics, it still doesn't "appeal to the eye." That's when the talent of the hand distinguishes the high-quality piece from the more mundane.

Two master embroiderers offered further opinions about the importance of counting fabric threads as the embroiderer covers them with khamak stitches.

It is very important to count the threads. Not counting the fabric is like walking on a bumpy road. When you are walking on a bumpy road, you might not fall all of the time, but when your foot hits a rock that will make you fall. You have to get up and start over. With khamak when you make a mistake, you have to open your entire work to the beginning and restart. You lose all the time you put into it. When you stitch by counting, it's like walking on a smooth, straight road.

On the other hand, a skilled master-level embroiderer can use her trained eye in place of precise counting:

One benefit of elevating yourself to the master level is that you can make the khamak look good without counting. That enables you to work on any type of fabric. When you cannot see the weave of a tightly woven fabric, and you are only dependent on counting, then you cannot work on that fabric. For the master, even if you cannot see to count the threads, you can still make the shape perfectly nice on a tightly woven fabric.

Cleanliness is another differentiating feature of high-quality khamak. Dust covers Kandahar streets and permeates its homes. When tightly woven fabrics are used as the base textiles for embroidery, the dust is likely to catch in the tightly executed stitches, resulting in a dirty-looking product. To offset this possibility, women baste fabric scraps from other sewing projects over the unworked sections of a scarf or shawl. The covering prevents the unworked sections from collecting dust. As one woman explained, "When our customers come to see our embroidery, they see no fault in our work—in the cleanliness, in the finishing. We are known for doing very clean khamak."

The women of Kandahar Treasure take great pride in their work and credit the organizational systems in place for delivering work on time and as promised to customers. As one woman summarized, "We get treated well here and with respect. So in response we do the best of our ability to produce the best work we can." Rangina continued, "The best embroiderers are constantly working to achieve perfection—this is a reflection of life. They are expected to deliver what the society, the family, the culture expect them to—a perfect life as others have defined it. Delivering that perfect life requires perfection in every detail."

CONFLICT NEGOTIATOR—
"BE LIKE HER."

KAMAR GUL'S STORY

When asked how she used her money from Kandahar Treasure, Kamar Gul replied, "I run my home with it. My entire household expenses from flour to soap, to notebooks, pens, and backpacks, I buy. Everything in my house I buy with my money." In addition to these formidable family responsibilities, Kamar Gul exerts influence within her Kandahar neighborhood and out to her rural village.

Kamar Gul arrived at Kandahar Treasure seven years ago as a widow whose husband and oldest son had been killed. After completing several embroidery orders in her home, Kamar Gul returned with beautiful, high-quality khamak. Recognizing her skill and potential, Rangina offered her a salaried position in the office, which allowed her to support her family with her work at Kandahar Treasure. Kamar Gul assessed that before she was widowed and moved to the city she would

not have been able to live on her own as she is now, supporting four daughters and three sons.

When living in the village, she remained secluded at home. She didn't have her husband's permission to go outside, yet she harbored a lifelong desire to help others. In the village, devoid of doctors and clinics, Kamar Gul attended to the sick and delivered babies when women came to her home. She said that upon moving to Kandahar city, "The wishes in my heart flourished. And now that I am seeing the world outside of my home, I've been able to learn and manage new things in life that have helped me to become who I am. I couldn't be who I am today if I hadn't left my home in the village."

All three sons are attending school in the city, as is her youngest daughter. Although Kamar Gul no longer has a husband to oversee her life, her sons still exert patriarchal influence in the household. When one of her sons believed his elder sister was too old to be going to school, he pulled her out. Today,

the daughter embroiders khamak at home. As a poor woman not owning a home, Kamar Gul has been forced to move from place to place, sometimes into neighborhoods unsafe for girls. Completing the paperwork for transferring schools and gaining entrance in new schools presents challenges for an illiterate woman. Because her nine-year-old daughter walks forty-five minutes to her current school, Kamar Gul is constantly worried. "Did she make it to school? Is she okay?" When asked if she would allow her son to pull her youngest daughter from fourth grade, Kamar Gul replied, "No… Even if I have to move out of the house, I won't let her not finish her school."

Kamar Gul serves as a negotiator for peace in her Kandahar neighborhood. She told of an incident two months ago when she heard men fighting outside her compound walls. Men screamed and yelled. She opened her door to see a man holding a knife ready to kill another neighbor. Kamar Gul immediately intervened to stop

the murder by inserting herself between the two men. Men of the neighborhood stood by, but no one else stepped forward to break up the fight.

Beyond her neighborhood, Kamar Gul offers her negotiation skills back at her village where she mediates family disputes—husbands with wives, and mothers-in-law with daughters-in-laws. Displaying exemplary bravery, she intervened when the Taliban took over her nephew's home as a hub for their wartime conflict. The commander kicked the nephew, his wife, and six children, some of whom were babies, out of the house. When the nephew went to Kamar Gul with the plaint, "We have no place to go," she made a visit to meet the Talibs stationed in her nephew's home.

Taking tea, she sat down for a conversation with the men holding kalashnikov weapons at their sides. She began by reminding the men that they were Muslims, Pashtuns, and Kandaharis, with all that implies for cultural traditions and treatment

Women shrouded in burqas stand in contrast to young men and boys who have adopted Western dress.

of others. Continuing, she laid out her case, asking the Taliban men to be the judge. Kamar Gul explained that her nephew had a family of small children. He could not move to the city; he knew little of urban life and had no skills for earning an income in the city. The nephew cultivated a small plot of land in the village for his family's livelihood. Yet now his home was taken from him. What was he to do? Although she never received a direct answer from the commander, he eventually stood up and ordered his men to get out of the house. As he left, the commander offered words of apology for the trouble they had caused the family.

Over the years, as Kamar Gul has become recognized for her mediation skills, men in her Kandahar neighborhood and in her village now hold her up as an example to their wives: "Be like her. Be like her in solving problems." Rangina reflected on Kamar Gul's transformation from a quiet, serious woman arriving at Kandahar Treasure to her role today as an outspoken Taliban mediator. "This hasn't ended the war or our problems, but a simple woman has been able to negotiate for her community solutions to problems for which others believed there was no solution."

SEVEN

APPROACHING *the* FUTURE
with PRIDE *and* APPREHENSION

*Social entrepreneurs demonstrate the power of
building things instead of destroying them.
They are addressing many of the causes
of today's global instability: Lack of education, lack of
women's rights, destruction of the environment, poverty.*

David Bornstein, *How to Change the World*

Rangina entered the embroidery room to find the women agitating about yet another distressing government action. She asked, "What can you do about it?" Within minutes the women talked about taking charge, ousting the current government in a coup, and establishing roles for themselves in the new administration. Kamar Gul took over as Governor and appointed women to cabinet positions according to their skills. The cleaning lady became the Mayor as she would keep the city clean. One of the women who loved learning assumed the role as Head of Education. Another woman who complained constantly about electricity outages became the Head of the Electricity Department, and so on. Excitement permeated the room in lively discussion for over thirty minutes. At the end, they sighed, woke up from their dream, and resumed their embroidery. For these women, Kandahar Treasure had become a safe workshop where they could talk and dream about a future. Later, Rangina reflected on this burst of energy, "The fact that they can even dream about this is something that never happened before. With time and with stability, there is the possibility of change. Our moments of dreaming about the future is that hope."

The world has invested in Afghanistan for several decades but still has little understanding of the people and their culture. Women are depicted in the media as weak, voiceless victims of violence. In contrast, the women of Kandahar Treasure are actively creating change in a country portrayed by journalists as the worst place in the world to be a woman. Over the past fourteen years, this

Stitching together has given the women of Kandahar Treasure an opportunity to develop relationships and an outspokenness that wouldn't have been possible if they had remained confined to their family compounds.

safe enclave has offered more than 500 women the opportunity to create new answers for their lives in a culture where their proscriptive destinies were set by men. Despite familial, economic, and social obstacles, they are redefining the boundaries of their lives through embroidery. Rangina stated, "We have a group of strong women who are speaking loud and clear to us through their textiles. It is our duty to raise their voice."

WIDOWHOOD AND KANDAHAR TREASURE

Kandahar Treasure is respected within Kandahar for providing working opportunities for a significant number of widows. Income earned by widows in Kandahar Treasure is particularly noteworthy, given that widowhood can condemn a woman to a tragic life. Ironically, widowhood attracts a special kind of mercy and attention within the practice of the Muslim faith in Afghanistan. Giving of charity to the needy stands as one of the five pillars of Islam. Historically, Afghans have prioritized their charity to widows and orphans. Yet even with the charitable assis-

tance that some widows receive, life is difficult for most. Alone, widows face many financial and social challenges. Without husbands, responsibilities for supporting numerous children are multiplied; begging as a last resort is not uncommon.

Despite these challenges, some widows can achieve a level of independence in Afghanistan that married women do not. Not having a husband to report to or to ask permission from, widows can accomplish greater change in their lives than women with husbands. The most evident examples of women as change agents in the network of Kandahar Treasure members are the widowed mothers. These mothers are drawing new boundaries for their daughters by allowing them a future that they could not dream of with a father dictating their lives.

The popular phrase that "money is power" is clearly evident among the women working with Kandahar Treasure. Having access to work and having the ability to earn their own money enables women to redefine their own boundaries. Financial independence is the foundation of sustainable development for women in Kandahar, as it is in much of the developing world.

Fareba is a strong and wise manager of Kandahar Treasure, standing in for Rangina when necessary.

A SOCIAL ENTREPRENEUR LEADS THE WAY

Social entrepreneurs target a neglected segment of humanity that lacks the means or clout to achieve transformation on their own. Social entrepreneurs apply inspiration, creativity, action, fortitude, and often courage toward change that brings future benefit to an excluded group. This definition succinctly describes Rangina Hamidi as a *social entrepreneur* and the work of Kandahar Treasure as a *social enterprise* aimed at decreasing marginalization of women in Afghanistan. Rangina and Kandahar Treasure work in a country of ongoing violence, insecurity, and economic exigency. Yet the characteristics common to successful social entrepreneurs worldwide apply in Afghanistan for redefining opportunities for Afghan women. How Kandahar Treasure has evolved as a social enterprise under Rangina's leadership offers insights to other artisan enterprises and their leaders.

Starting with an obsession. Bornstein noted that "social entrepreneurs at some point in their lives get it into their heads that it is up to them to solve a particular problem, often triggered by an event. They become obsessed with the idea." Rangina's visit to the Afghan refugee camps in 1998 triggered her obsession. She could not stand to see the people suffering. She witnessed monetary donations from the international community quickly disappear as refugees used the funds to meet immediate basic needs. No long-term benefits ensued. Rangina became consumed with how women could build capacity for change in their lives, while decreasing their dependency on men.

Attending to the context. Successful social entrepreneurs listen carefully to their environment. They grasp what is happening within a society's daily economic, social, and political routines. A deep awareness of cultural nuances undergirds this understanding. For Kandahar Treasure, Rangina drew on her enmeshment in Afghan culture, coupled with her life as a Western educated Afghan American, for accomplishing two important goals—identifying an organizational leader and promoting schooling for girls.

As Rangina looked to a time when she might no longer reside permanently in Kandahar, selecting and mentoring a workshop manager assumed priority. She needed a leader who was committed to khamak revival and could gain the respect of the women for furthering the vision. The future manager must be available to work long, often flexible hours to meet business deadlines. As few Afghan women had previous management experience, the manager needed to be willing to learn this new role. In sum, Rangina wanted a manager who did not fit the cultural norm for a Kandahari woman, whose time was consumed by caring for a large household. Yet the woman's public demeanor needed to be respectful of Afghan culture. She should not call unwanted negative attention to herself or to the organization.

Fareba, a woman in her mid-thirties, met the requirements. She was divorced; did not have children; lived with her father, mother, and brothers; and had no household responsibilities. Rangina recalled embroidery orders Fareba had completed at home. The khamak she returned to the workshop was of the finest quality with great attention to detail. Rangina assessed that Fareba might transfer those qualities to a managerial role in setting high standards for the women and in gaining their esteem. Initially reluctant as she had never worked in an office, Fareba consulted her parents for advice. The parents encouraged her to give the work a try.

Fareba's life without household responsibilities allowed her freedom to devote considerable time to Kandahar Treasure, even staying late as needed. As anticipated, Fareba established procedures to help the women improve their work, "If I have to turn down a woman's work, I explain and show her why the work does not meet the standards. I make her see her mistakes. I don't just tell her that she made a mistake and that's it."

By joining Rangina on trips to India, Fareba broadened her perspective on craft development and marketing in other countries. In 2016, after urging from Rangina to attend night school, she completed her high school certificate. Fareba is clearly aware that had she married at a young age and had a large family, she would not be making independent decisions about her life. She said, "There would be someone telling me where to go, where not to go, what to do, what not to do, what to wear, what not to wear." She continued, "In our traditional way of marrying, the family—husband, mother-in-law, father-in-law, sister-in-law—snatches the little courage you have as an individual from you. Once you are working, you find the courage that you are capable and can do the work. My family is proud of what I am doing—what I have become that I hadn't become before."

Mentoring. In addition to choosing a manager, Rangina supported schooling for girls from her insider perspective as well. Her Women's Studies courses at the University of Virginia had instilled the feminist argument that education for girls is a basic human right. Women of Kandahar Treasure recognized their lack of education had greatly limited their opportunities in life. Gradually some of the women started sending their daughters to school—a brave initiative that Rangina applauded. Rangina and other Afghan mentors have taken a measured approach for working with the girls. As non-family members, the mentors have already crossed a boundary of providing guidance to young girls in households where they are not members. She advised girls, "In the process of getting yourself educated, don't do other smaller things that will attract negative attention. Be careful in the choices you make. You've already made a big one." Rangina works from a philosophy that change coming from within the culture, one step at a time, has the potential to sustain itself.

Rangina recalled an incident from her past that sparked her philosophy for how to support education of young girls in Afghanistan. A leading politician invited her to join him in attending an all-male voter registration meeting. As she sat quietly, dressed completely in black, she was introduced as the granddaughter of a respected elder from Afghanistan's past. One man spoke up, saying that he was aware that she was educated in the United States, but yet he noted that she acted very respectful of Afghan culture. Rangina recalled, "That moment made me feel like I was

on a pedestal of educated women in Afghanistan. I saw that I needed to act and present myself in a manner that would not be taken as 'this is not what we want.' Rather this is what an educated woman can be like." She knew that men felt threatened from what they had recently seen, particularly from the Communist regime that forced women to go out in public without a head scarf or to attend school against the will of male family members. Men's experiences with educated girls giving up their culture permeated their viewpoints. This man's affirmation of Rangina confirmed her belief that change for women could occur if done carefully and strategically.

Drawing on personal networks. In addition to a strong grounding in Afghan culture, Rangina drew on personal and motivational qualities common to social entrepreneurs worldwide. Rangina cited patience, perseverance, and drive as essential to her work. She was well aware that expanding women's roles to include work with Kandahar Treasure meant shifting long-held patriarchal attitudes and alleviating fear from men within the society. From the beginning, the organization focused on a Kandahari tradition that is within women's purview, "Khamak is our activity. This is what we are doing. It's non-threatening—almost benign. We don't touch politics. We don't touch sensitive parts of society. We use a tradition that we are known for and we are using that to make money."

Visioning with flexibility. Successful social entrepreneurs hold tight to a vision for change, but exhibit flexibility in how to carry out their important work. Willingness to self-correct along the way helps entrepreneurs remain procedurally nimble. Rangina's vision for Kandahar Treasure—reviving a textile tradition and empowering women—remained steadfast in her mind. The plan for reaching the goal changed as Rangina self-corrected the organization's business practices when Afghan insecurity heightened and as her knowledge of consumer product preferences expanded.

Originally, Rangina planned to visit the homes of all women asking to join Kandahar Treasure. Visits helped her to meet the family, observe conditions of the home,

Creating educational opportunities for girls is one of Kandahar's greatest challenges. Before the Soviet occupation, girls and women had much more freedom. Today, they must be careful to observe cultural imperatives while seeking a future for themselves.

All the challenges, hopes, fears, and determination are reflected in Rangina's eyes as she contemplates the future of Kandahar Treasure.

and assess the women's need for work. However, when insecurity on the streets increased in late 2006, visits to the homes of women became dangerous. Word-of-mouth referrals from current Kandahar Treasure embroiderers replaced the visits to potential members' home.

Product colors cycled in and out as Rangina participated in international markets. The locally preferred pastel color palette veered first toward very bright hues, still favored locally, but then eventually refocused to a less saturated color range preferable abroad. Embroiderers found Western women's preference for black fabrics in fashion apparel to be confusing. For them, wearing a large black head covering symbolized a serious Muslim woman, not a fashion choice. However, including some black items in the product mix for markets in the United States contributed to sales. Additionally, with more opportunities to market its products to both national and international markets, Kandahar Treasure has been able to differentiate products based on the market needs. Product aesthetics and type differ between those for the Afghan market and others for their non-Afghan customers.

Drawing on professional networks. Speaking multiple languages—Pashto, Dari, Hindi, Urdu, English—has allowed Rangina to work from a strong foothold in both Afghan and United States societies. Not only can she communicate with the Afghan women with whom she works but also she has accessed networks for entrepreneurial guidance in the West that have been critical to Kandahar Treasure's growth. Through these networks, Rangina gained basic business operational skills. She talked with thousands of customers in the United States, exchanging her story of Kandahar Treasure with the customers' input on product design and preference. Through a stream of invited presentations in large public settings, she gained confidence and expertise for presenting a hopeful story for Afghan women to the world.

To date, the social enterprise literature has not documented artisan organizations as a form of social enterprise. Our assessment provides such documentation and serves as an example for comparison and contrast with other artisan organizations with social goals.

KANDAHAR TREASURE: Looking to the Future

In the Preface and Chapter 1 of this book, we posed questions as to why women would leave the protective boundaries of their homes and put their lives in danger in the streets as they traveled for work at Kandahar Treasure. We asked how they worked and prospered within the confining boundaries of a patriarchal society. The ensuing chapters have told the unfolding story of how, through the revival of khamak, women have acquired income-generating skills for enhancing their livelihood. Their earnings have contributed vital income for family survival in households where husbands could not find jobs or worked only sporadically. When asked how they used their earnings, women quickly and emphatically answered, "We feed our families."

Kandahar Treasure has fostered a safe, women-only working environment in which women's honor could be respected by men and the larger society. As the women have embroidered and tailored within a workplace respectful of Muslim practices and contributed to household expenses, they have earned recognition from their household members and gained strength to make decisions in the form of *new answers* for their lives and the lives of their children.

Rangina and the women of Kandahar Treasure take great pride in their accomplishments. Rangina says, "To change the face of Kandahar was not part of my business plan. But over the years it gives me a tremendous amount of pride knowing that on the one hand Kandahar is dangerous and full of violence, but at the same time we are creating beauty, we're creating art, we're creating textiles that have a longer history in my country than the more recent negative images and perceptions. I'm helping to build that society of construction, not destruction. We're not there yet, so there is still tremendous drive."

Entrepreneurial journeys inevitably hit roadblocks along the way and face threats for the future. Kandahar Treasure is no exception as it seeks to create change in a patriarchal society that resists embracing new ideas. While it has great potential to grow into a thriving social enterprise, there are daily struggles that create apprehension about its future.

Afghanistan as a whole is a threatened nation, and Kandahar Province in particular faces serious risks to its security. Politically, this important province carries the weight of political shifts within the country. The fact that Kandahar was, and to an extent remains, the de facto capital of the Taliban movement does not serve its people well. The political unrest in the province has frightened many away from Kandahar. In addition, the tribal politics of Afghanistan since 2002 have contributed to the label for Kandahar as one of the least favored regions in the country in which to live and work.

Continuing insurgency attacks threaten security on the streets. Infrastructure of roads remains in shambles; travel outside the city requires long hours on roadways filled with potholes. Insecurity on the streets and risky travel not only interfere with daily operations for transporting raw materials and finished goods but threaten the positive outlook for Kandahar Treasure employees who risk their lives merely coming to work each day.

The insecurity of the country also discourages potential designers and development workers from coming and working first-hand with the artisans. Several leading U.S. designers, whose firms follow socially-responsible practices compatible with Kandahar Treasure's approach to its work, have offered to collaborate with Kandahar Treasure on new product development. However, the designers are fearful about traveling to Afghanistan for the face-to-face learning that is essential to sustainable new product design for international markets. Without on-the-ground access by designers to the embroidery processes, working conditions, and cultural parameters of women's lives, designers will not be able to fully appreciate or understand the craft or how to sustainably collaborate with the artisans for incorporating khamak embroidery into new and modern designs.

Threats to Kandahar Treasure and the tradition of khamak embroidery go unrecognized at Afghanistan's national level. The government of Afghanistan, unlike

Revival of the khamak tradition depends on two essential participants in the marketplace—the artists who produce the art, and the demand of consumers for this art.

many developing countries such as India, has no policy of promoting Afghan crafts, either financially or culturally. The Afghan government struggles to define itself, and attention to what may appear to be small but important ideas and concepts does not seem to be on its agenda. But Kandahar Treasure's track record provides evidence that it is precisely these small projects that will aid in developing Afghanistan, and particularly its women and children.

Revival of the khamak tradition depends on two essential participants in the marketplace—the artists who produce the art, and the demand of consumers for this art. If women's roles in society are to be broadened, promoting girls to be educated and to advance in their studies is essential. Yet greater education for girls serves as a double-edged sword for the future of khamak. With girls devoting more hours to schooling and eventual participation in public life, khamak will likely languish as girls have little time to learn or practice the art. However, girls who are tied to a traditional, home-based lifestyle where embroidery revival thrives, will forego opportunities to acquire education as a basic human right. Khamak revival may not yet be threatened, but as more and more girls attend schools, khamak embroidery could face an inevitable demise.

Additionally, machine-made replicas of baby sets, trousseau textiles, and men's shirts, at a fraction of the cost of the fine hand-made embroidery, have already saturated Afghan retail shops and markets. In the unstable economy of Afghanistan with many men out of work, it becomes difficult to negatively judge its consumers when they invest in an affordable machine-embroidered tunic over an expensive handmade piece, even when they know the cultural value of the handmade alternative.

Robust domestic customer demand for khamak products has faded in recent years. Closure of the Kandahar Treasure retail shop at the NATO military base in Kandahar in 2014 was a severe financial blow to the women artisans who depended on the regular income from sales of their products. In addition, sales at their two local shops are stagnant.

Several actions are underway to assess risks to Kandahar Treasure's survival. First, working with an international business consultant, Rangina is reviewing organizational and accounting practices for ways to create operational and staffing efficiencies. Personally, Rangina finds that reducing work hours or eliminating office staff positions to be extremely painful. To do so, Kandahar Treasure eliminates essential income for women who have no other earning opportunities and on whom their families are solely or heavily dependent for food to eat each day.

Second, until the Afghan economy improves, a search for new external market opportunities has assumed priority with a focus on expansion to additional international sales venues and collaboration with international designers. Conscious of Kandahar Treasure's financial emergency and apprehensive about their future, in 2016 the women unanimously agreed to forego the lunch provided for them in the workplace. Despite these challenges and apprehensions, the women artisans at Kandahar Treasure are still willing to take on the challenges, even in very trying times. Holding immense pride in their accomplishments, the women remain tenacious in continuing to mold and shape their lives. Kandahar Treasure's future depends on how the continuing Afghan insurgency evolves, the economy stabilizes, organizational efficiencies are enacted, and the international community responds to Kandahar Treasure's overtures for greater design investment and market opportunities.

Khamak embroidery on black fabric makes a stunning fashion statement for women in the West but is a perplexing choice for Afghan women who associate black with widowhood. Kandahar Treasure takes care to follow market trends.

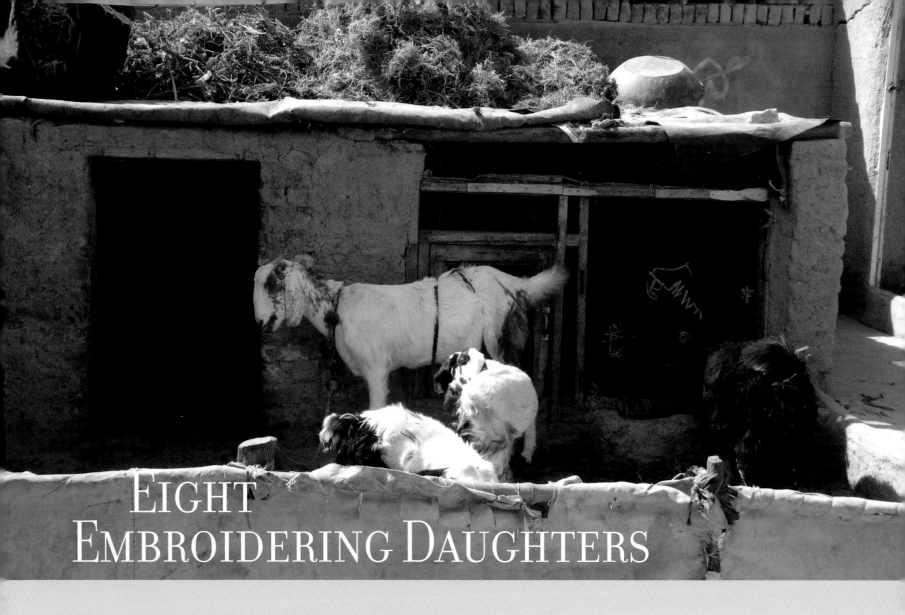

EIGHT
EMBROIDERING DAUGHTERS

AMINA'S TALE

Our driver navigated down a narrow, rutted alleyway and deposited us at the unmarked metal door of a mud-brick compound. We were arriving at Amina's house unannounced and one day earlier than her invitation. Security was threatened once again in Kandahar, as a young Afghan woman had been assassinated that morning on her way to work. Nerves frayed, doubts raised about whom to trust. Rangina wanted to protect Amina's family from the possible risk of hosting two foreign women and herself for tea.

As we entered, two young girls rushed forward to remove our burqas and hang them on wall pegs. Soapsuds from early morning wash

Embroidering from dawn to dusk keeps Amina's family fed. As the girls grow older and go to their own households, family income will decline.

Embroidery is only part of the work in Amina's compound. Tending livestock, making yogurt, and cooking for this large extended family are constant and critical tasks.

covered the ground near a water spigot in a corner of the courtyard. Goats roamed behind a low walled partition, eating their morning hay. Amina greeted us warmly and ushered us into a room reserved for receiving female guests. We would be safely out of sight from any men entering the compound. Stunning khamak textiles in violet and white decorated every wall and object in the small room, covering storage cases, sleeping mats, a sewing machine; and high on one wall, khamak protected the family's Quran. Floor and wall cushions on a bright red rug provided comfortable seating.

The room was engulfed immediately with women and girls—up to twenty at one time crammed together, some sitting two-deep around the walls ready for conversation and tea. Rangina and Amina initiated the traditional Afghan greeting of simultaneously offering back and forth phrases of welcome and inquiries about family and health. Daughters served Afghan green tea and placed individual plates of carefully arranged cookies at our feet. A box of tissues served as napkins. Three generations, from grandmother to granddaughters, joined in animated conversation, often talking simultaneously. When Rangina explained we were there to learn more about khamak, Amina quickly responded, "For us women, khamak is our biggest asset in life. Khamak is what we have. If everyone became skilled in reading and writing, then who would do khamak?"

Amina, thirty-eight, lives surrounded by a houseful of children. Married at twelve, she gave birth at fourteen to her first child, a son.

A Quran cover is only one of many khamak-embroidered textiles that grace Amina's home.

Two years later he died, along with his uncle, in a wartime attack. One by one, births of eleven daughters followed, yet Amina remained hopeful for another son. Today, her dreams are fulfilled with her three youngest children, all sons.

Wartime tragedy and sadness permeate family stories in Afghanistan. Amina's family is no exception. Near the time of her first child's death, Amina's husband stepped on a land mine and lost his foot. Catastrophe continued when a married daughter died in a horrific accident. Living with her in-laws, the daughter was unaware that a brother-in-law was making munitions secretly in the house. Amina, quietly weeping, shared that one day the munitions blew up, simultaneously killing Amina's favorite daughter and her nine-month old baby. Amina also cares for six orphan children, four girls and two boys, whose father was killed. Their mother, Amina's sister, has remarried and moved away. Today, with two of Amina's oldest daughters now married and living with their in-laws, eight daughters and three sons remain at home. The six orphans fill the household with a total of seventeen children.

Conversation in the room roamed over a variety of topics from the importance of khamak, to discussion of household expenses, and viewpoints on foreigners. Amina explained that she and all eight daughters embroider. "As long as there is daylight we're doing khamak. The sun rises. The sun sets. We're all working." Stitch by tiny stitch, the girls sit together completing the fine, intricate motifs. Their mother, wearing glasses, embroiders shawls with their larger designs. Amina remains steadfast in not buying a television for fear it will draw her daughters' attention away from their embroidery. None of the girls have been to school. Yet Zarghona, a teenage daughter, offered that khamak "is my signature, my writing, my pen." Since she was not allowed to be educated, she sees her khamak as her expression, as her writing to the world.

Amina explains, "Meeting all of our expenses is with our needles." Although Amina's husband can still work, his income merely covers their monthly rent of 4,000 afghanis (about $58 US) and one bag of flour at 1,500 afghanis (about $22). The family needs four bags of flour a month to make the requisite bread served for every meal. Other food purchases include rice, cooking oil, sugar, vegetables, and tea—a constant companion for the girls and their mother to drink as they embroider. Purchases of medicine, clothing, shoes, and other household needs round out the monthly expenses. The family's goats provide milk and yogurt. When asked why she has goats rather than cows, Amina asserted that cows are "bigger, harder to take care of, and take more time and attention."

Amina estimates they spend 25,000 afghanis (about $365) per year on household expenses, exclusive of flour. "We do all of that with our needles and our hands." Trust generated over time between this family of loyal embroiderers and Kandahar Treasure is such that when times are tough for meeting monthly expenses of Amina's large family, Kandahar Treasure advances money to her prior to the completion of embroidery projects. Although the Afghan government offers financial programs to aid the handicapped and orphans, Amina has no time to run around to the various government offices and seek help in applying for this funding.

Animated discussion segued into experiences with foreigners.

How soon will this happy grandson outgrow his beautiful khamak tunic? It doesn't matter. Every little boy must have one. OPPOSITE: Khamak textiles cover every item in the "women's room" in Amina's home.

One woman shared that her son works in an office frequented by women foreigners. He expressed surprise to see the foreign women properly covered from head to toe. He considered their attire as a sign of respect for Afghan culture. Other women joined in, expressing disdain for "our own women" who, once they see a little of foreign life, lose their traditions and culture. Directing her comments to Rangina, one woman offered, "If you were not educated, how could we have this bridge between people who don't know our language and we don't know their language? We need people to do this." Yet Rangina countered that Afghans who work with foreigners are vulnerable, as they are viewed by the Taliban as "the eyes and ears" of the enemy. Targeting these Afghan workers for assassination is considered a first step toward eradicating the enemy.

As our visit came to an end, conversation turned to family matters. Clearly, Amina is proud of her daughters, all of whom show strong facial resemblance to their mother and echo her quiet strength. Each of the eight embroidering daughters contributes essential earnings to this family's precarious livelihood. As we prepared to leave, Amina shared her harbored fear that when she dies, God will tell her that she overworked her body and the bodies of her daughters.

KANDAHAR TREASURE— CREATING *a* FUTURE

Pashtun tradition dictates that men provide for all the financial needs of their households. Yet in a country with high rates of unemployment and poorly remunerated, part-time work, many men and their families live on the margins. In this dire context, income earned by the women of Kandahar Treasure provides essential resources for families to survive. For most of the women, all of their earnings go toward covering household expenses. One woman enumerated: flour, cooking oil, rice, matches, sugar, tea, candy, food, clothes, headscarves, and shoes. Women pay rent and some have saved for dowries to "buy" brides for their brothers and sons.

Kandahar Treasure women suffer from a variety of health issues such as malnutrition, depression, headaches, malaria, typhoid fever, and tuberculosis. Failing eyesight commonly occurs as the women embroider the small stitches, often under poor lighting. Women use their earnings for medicines or for professional healthcare for themselves and their families. Occasionally, a woman saves enough to take a family member to Pakistan, where doctors can provide specialized treatment for a daughter's eye problems or carry out tests for diagnosing why a child has become increasingly ill and lethargic. One woman with three daughters recognized the stiffness and back pain arising from her daughters' embroidering all day while sitting on the floor. She now organizes the household chores so each girl rotates two days of physical activity performing household tasks with four days of embroidering in a seated position on the floor.

Women also contribute money toward helping their children experience a better life than they themselves have lived. Paying for a child to attend a private school enhances the child's future. Several women have freed their daughters from the hardships and sorrow of early marriages. One woman's fifteen-year-old daughter had been promised to an elderly man in exchange for a large loan the woman's husband had received from the man when the girl was only three years old. As the marriage approached, the daughter vowed to commit suicide on the

A woman holds a baby in one hand and holds the other up in prayer as she joins hundreds of other women praying for peace to commemorate International Women's Day in Kandahar, in 2009.

day of the wedding. Fortunately, between what the mother saved and borrowed over a two-year period, she paid off the man on the day he arrived to take the daughter away. Another woman proudly explained that the money her daughters earned from khamak was so essential to the household's functioning that it had prevented her husband from marrying off three of their daughters when they were very young. Instead, earnings from khamak helped the girls avoid the harsh life of an early marriage and bearing children as young teenagers.

For women in dire economic straits, with no sources of income, begging or borrowing becomes a last resort. Rangina explained, "Borrowing is a huge dilemma, especially for widows. People borrow because they don't have food to feed their children. And then there is no way to pay it back. If you cannot pay it back, you cannot borrow money from that person again. That can break relationships, especially if it is borrowing from family or friends. People go around exposing your reputation to others. It makes you look shameful." Kandahar Treasure tries to break that dependency on borrowing, "Pretty much what Kandahar Treasure is doing is providing food for the day. For most women, it is not allowing them to buy homes or set aside savings. It is only helping households to survive."

GAINING RESPECT IN THE HOME

Human well-being encompasses more than improved economic livelihood. Emotional health and social empowerment contribute to increased self-respect, confidence, and courage. Two women talked of how doing khamak contributed to inner peace in a war-torn country. One woman explained that concentrating on her khamak takes her mind away from all the crazy things in life that surround her every day—all the foolish things she could get involved in with friends, family, and neighbors. Another woman said that when her mother found her embroidering late at night, she told her, "When you die, God will tell you that you have misused these hands. You are working too much and abusing them." But the daughter replied that doing khamak calms her and helps take her attention away from the horrible problems of life. Rather than thinking about these problems when she cannot go to sleep, she put her hands and mind to good use.

Women of Kandahar Treasure have created a community of support and friendship that not only strengthens them as individuals, but also empowers them beyond the workplace. One woman who comes daily to the workshop elaborated, "Here we've become like classmates in a school. So, if one of us doesn't show up on a day, we get worried. We wonder what's wrong with her. Is she okay? We try to call each other to follow up. We really do care about each other."

Beyond the workplace, women experience new respect within their families as a result of their Kandahar Treasure earnings. This new deference is particularly noteworthy in a culture where men feel belittled by asking women for money. One woman explained,

> When my father was alive, when he was not as old and I was young, no one respected me, including my father. But when I started working and bringing money home, my old father started to respect me. He would even ask me, 'How are you doing daughter?' He would tell the other children to not bother me, as I was tired and coming from work. And now that he has passed on, my brothers continue that behavior. When I go home from work, they ask me 'How are you?' They would not have done that if I wasn't working.

The wife of a rickshaw driver, an expert embroiderer who works in her home, told how her husband acknowl-edged that her khamak earnings bring more income into the household than his driving a rickshaw. The husband started helping with the household to give her more time for her khamak. Recently, when asked how she completed and returned a khamak order so quickly, she laughed, "He took care of the kids, he cleaned the house, he even cooked to allow me to finish this. We are desperate for money, as he has been sick and cannot drive the rickshaw."

In another example, Rangina recalled the first day that Paindo arrived at Kandahar Treasure. She was sick, shy, and depressed. She barely looked up from her lap. Although Kandahar Treasure gave her work to do, completing the embroidery at home in a household of boys wasn't fun. Eventually, she received permission from her father to work regularly at the workshop. Over the years she acquired skills for cutting and preparing the fabrics. She found her niche in organizing and overseeing the supplies, "I love fabrics. I wish I could just sit in that room and be with the fabrics on my own. But of course I know there is other work to be done." Some ten years later, she's outgoing and the confident leader of her household. She transformed from a girl with no power in her family to now talking confidently with the men. The entire household depends on her steady income, derived from her courage for going out of the home each day for work at Kandahar Treasure.

REVIVING A TRADITION: "It defines who we are."

Decades of war in Afghanistan disrupted families, left men disabled and women widowed, and disturbed economic systems for family support—all challenges for reviving the khamak embroidery tradition. Little time or energy was left for families living amidst conflict and deprivation to pass down textile practices.

Reviving a textile tradition builds on embracing a vision, creating standards for continual quality improvement, earning recognition from within and outside the

Artist's CHOICE

Excellence of design and execution are the hallmarks of Kandahar Treasure work.

society, and establishing a lifeline for the future. In the early days of Kandahar Treasure, women failed to appreciate the value of their khamak embroidery. As one woman said, "It's just stitches and we've been doing this forever." Repeatedly, Rangina shared the organization's vision of reviving the rare and unique embroidery of Kandahar and empowering the women in the process. Over and over she said to the women, "This is important, this is incredible, this is art, this is history, this is culture—we women are the bearers of this work."

Not all the women bought into the vision immediately. When Rangina returned from her BPeace training in New York, she shared the new name of Kandahar Treasure with the women and asked their opinions. Paindo looked up and asked with a frown on her face, "What's so treasurable about all those stitches we have to do?" Rangina encouraged the women that among the women of Afghanistan, Kandahari women are the only ones who can do this fine embroidery. Men can never do this work. To reinforce the vision, Rangina has taken some of the women to India to visit the Craft Museum in New Delhi. There they have seen how other countries are advancing their crafts. The women returned and shared their observations with other members. Today, when Paindo goes to public meetings, she proudly tells people, "I am a member of Kandahar Treasure."

Years ago, when Rangina first assumed sole responsibility for the Afghans for Civil Society (ACS) embroidery project, the women produced mediocre quality work for which they were paid, without question. There was no pressure to improve their work. Their attitude reflected an atmosphere after the war years, where "it's good enough" permeated multiple spheres of workforce philosophy. Creating a workshop culture of continual quality improvement, with evolving rewards, took time. Whereas in the earlier days, Kandahar Treasure would pay an embroiderer half of the expected price for a khamak of mid-range quality, today they only accept products of the highest quality. Evidence of their museum-quality work derives from one of their finest pieces being exhibited in New

Human well-being encompasses more than improved economic livelihood. Emotional health and social empowerment contribute to increased self-respect, confidence, and courage.

Mexico's Museum of International Folk Art, the premier folk art museum in the world.

Within Kandahar, a well-dressed Afghan man wears a khamak-embroidered shirt when out with other men. While women take pride in creating a new design for a man's tunic, they will never hear directly the compliments their men receive when in public wearing the newly embroidered garment. Yet the fact that embroidering a fine shirt for a husband, brother, or son brings honor to the family encourages women's continued participation in the art. In addition, Kandahar Treasure embroidery is sought out for custom orders of wedding trousseaus or baby sets among women who do not embroider. Were the khamak embroidery not so fundamental to Kandahari life, reviving the tradition likely would have been more difficult.

Abroad, as Rangina has taken the khamak to international markets and participated in in-home sales, she has learned that customers recognize and care about the craftsmanship of the finely counted stitches. Buyers applaud the neatly finished edges and even fringe of the scarves and shawls. Customer response and accompanying sales encourage the women back in Afghanistan that they are doing something important. Afghans living in the United States express pride that "khamak has traveled across the ocean to be part of Kandahari women's lives for special occasions in America." Although the art of khamak is no longer done in the United States, the Kandahari women there identify closely with it.

Slowly over time the Afghan women have bought into the Kandahar Treasure vision for reviving khamak. They have witnessed that their work is something valuable, not just because of the money they earned, but because of the way their art is used in Afghan society. As one woman noted, "Khamak is our history. It defines who we are."

Sustaining a textile tradition for the future demands commitment to teaching the high-quality practices established by the women of Kandahar Treasure. Malalai, a young, energetic, and creative master artist said, "It's just like teachers and students in first grade, when students don't have much knowledge. By the time that student graduates from twelfth grade, she will have acquired a lot of knowledge. Similarly with khamak, I see it as a talent. I have graduated in that talent. I have acquired all the knowledge to become a master. When I come up with new designs, techniques, new work, I am a teacher to the girls around me, just like a teacher in school is teaching students to read and write." Malalai's vision offers hope for the future of khamak as a living art in Kandahar society.

High-quality khamak embroidery requires a range of skills that go beyond reading and math. It is a special kind of literacy.

References

CHAPTER 1

Epigraph: **Louis Dupree,** *Afghanistan*, p. 250.

Page 20: **Graham-Harrison, Emma.** (March 7, 2014). "Afghanistan still one of the worst places to be a woman, says EU Ambassador." *The Guardian*. www.theguardian. com/world/2014/mar/07/hamid-karzai-afghanistan-women-eu-mellbin

Page 20: **Trondheim, Oscar.** (July 28, 2015). "The 10 Worst Countries for Women in 2015". *Viral Thread*. www.viral-thread.com/the-10-worst-countries-for-women-in-2015/

Page 20: **United Nations Development Programme.** (2015). Human Development Index. http://hdr.undp.org/en/2015-report

HUMAN DEVELOPMENT INDICATORS

RANK	COUNTRY	HUMAN DEVELOPMENT INDEX (HDI)	FEMALE YEARS OF SCHOOL	MALE YEARS OF SCHOOL	FEMALE INCOME	MALE INCOME	GENDER DEVELOPMENT Index (GDI)
1	Norway	.944	12.7	12.5	57,100	72,825	.996
8	U.S.	.915	13.0	12.9	43,054	63,158	.995
14	U.K.	.907	12.9	13.2	27,259	51,628	.965
39	Saudi Arabia	.837	7.8	9.3	20.094	77.044	.901
72	Turkey	.761	6.7	8.5	10,024	27,645	.902
74	Mexico	.756	8.2	8.8	10,233	22,252	.943
84	Peru	.734	8.5	9.6	8,040	13,977	.947
108	Egypt	.690	5.4	7.7	4,928	16,049	.868
121	Iraq	.654	5.1	7.7	4,270	23,515	.787
130	India	.609	3.6	7.2	2,116	8,656	.795
145	Kenya	.548	5.9	7.3	2,255	3,270	.913
147	Pakistan	.538	3.1	6.2	1,450	8.100	.726
163	Rwanda	.483	3.2	4.3	1,312	1,612	.957
171	Afghanistan	.465	1.2	5.1	506	3,227	.600
188	Niger	.348	0.8	2.0	491	1,319	.720

[1] Countries included for comparison are nations that experienced recent wars, are highly regarded for excellence in textile folk art, have significant Muslim populations, and/or provide contrasts among less- developed to more-developed countries.

[2] The Human Development Index (HDI), generated by the United Nations Development Programme, measures average achievement in key dimensions of human development: experiencing a long and healthy life, being knowledgeable and having a decent standard of living. The health dimension is assessed by life expectancy at birth. The education dimension is measured by mean years of schooling for adults aged 25. The standard of living dimension is measured by gross national income per capita. Indicators are for 2015 and accessed from www.hdr.undp.org

[3] A new indicator in 2015, the Gender Development Index (GDI), illuminates gaps in human development between the genders using the same indicators—health, knowledge, and living standards as for the HDI. The GDI is a direct measure of gender differentiation showing the female HDI as a percentage of the male HDI.

References

CHAPTER 1 (continued)
Page 23: **Abrahams, Jessica.** (July 18, 2014). "The war widows of Afghanistan." Prospect: *The Leading Magazine of Ideas.* http://www.prospectmagazine.co.uk/blogs/jessica-abrahams/the-war-widows-of-afghanistan

Page 28: **Padilla, Carmella.** (2013). *The Work of Art: Folk Artists in the 21st Century.* Santa Fe, NM: IFAA Media, p. 54.

CHAPTER 3
Epigraph: **Peter Sellars** *Textile Society of America Symposium.* 2014.

CHAPTER 4
Epigraph: **Tamin Ansary,** *West of Kabul, East of New York,* p. 17.

CHAPTER 5
Epigraph: **Carmella Padilla,** (2013). *The Work of Art: Folk Artists in the 21st Century.* Santa Fe, NM: IFAA Media, p. 54.

CHAPTER 7
Epigraph: **David Bornstein,** (2007). *How to Change the World. Social Entrepreneurs and the Power of New Ideas.* Oxford: Oxford University Press, p. 290

Page 141: **Roger L. Martin and Sally Osberg,** "Social Entrepreneurship: The Case for Definition." *Stanford Social Innovation Review.* www.ssir.org/articles/entry/social_entrepreneurship_the_case_for_definition

Page 141: **Bornstein, David.** (2007). *How to Change the World. Social Entrepreneurs and the Power of New Ideas.* Oxford: Oxford University Press, p. 126.

Bibliography

Ansary, Tamin. (2012). *Games without rules: The often interrupted history of Afghanistan.* New York: Public Affairs.

Ansary, Tamin. (2002). *West of Kabul, East of New York: An Afghan American story.* New York: Picador.

Bennett, Christopher G., Hamilton, Roy W., Ruiz, Alma, & Steinberger, Randi Malkin. (2012). *Order and Disorder: Alighiero Boetti by Afghan Women.* Los Angeles: Fowler Museum at UCLA.

Bornstein, David. (2007). *How to change the world. Social entrepreneurs and the power of new ideas.* Oxford: Oxford University Press.

Chambers, Robert. (1997). *Whose Reality Counts?: Putting the First Last.* London: Intermediate Technology Publications.

Coll, Steve. (2005). *Ghost wars: The secret history of the CIA, Afghanistan, and bin Laden, from the Soviet Invasion to September 10, 2001.* New York: Penguin Books.

Dupaigne, Bernard, Cousin, Françoise, Paiva, Mateo, & Paiva, Roland. (1993). *Afghan Embroidery.* Paris: Lahore Musée de l'Homme: U.N. High Commissioner for refugee: Fondation de France.

Dupree, Louis. (1980). *Afghanistan.* Princeton, NJ: Princeton University Press.

Gall, Carlotta. (2014). *The wrong enemy: American in Afghanistan, 2001-2014.* Boston: Houghton Mifflin Harcourt.

Martin, Roger L., & Osberg, Sally. (Spring, 2007). *Social entrepreneurship: The case for definition.* Stanford Social Innovation Review. Downloaded from ssir.org on August 14, 2016.

O'Brien, Tony, & Sullivan, Mike. (2008). *Afghan dreams: Young voices of Afghanistan.* New York: Bloomsbury.

Padilla, Carmella. (2013). *The Work of Art: Folk Artists in the 21st century.* Santa Fe, NM: IFAA Media.

Paine, Sheila. (1990). *Embroidered textiles: Traditional patterns from five continents.* New York: Rizzoli.

Paine, Sheila. (2006). *Embroidery from Afghanistan.* Seattle: University of Washington Press.

Skoll Centre for Social Entrepreneurship. (2016). *What is social entrepreneurship?* Oxford, England: University of Oxford. Available at www.skb.ox.ac.uk.

Photography Credits

All photographs are by **Paula Lerner** except for the following:

Joe Coca: pp. 56, 64, 66 (right), 67, 68, 69, 70–73, 115, 117, 119–124, 125 (bottom), 127, 130, 131, 147

Mary Littrell: pp. 23, 28, 31–39, 61–65, 66 (left), 74, 88–89, 91–92, 104-105, 107–108, 112, 116, 125 (top), 126, 128–129, 133, 139–140, 148–152, 154–155

Steve Simon: p. 51

Victor Zastolskiy: p. 82

Mian Khursheed: p. 85

Sanaullah Seiam: p. 161

Index